THE
INDISPENSABLE
GUIDE
to practically
EVERYTHING

Life After Death &
Heaven and Hell

THE
INDISPENSABLE
GUIDE
to practically
EVERYTHING

Life After Death &
Heaven and Hell

BRYAN McANALLY

Guideposts
New York, New York

The Indispensable Guide to Practically Everything: Life After Death & Heaven and Hell

ISBN 13: 978-0-8249-4773-6

Published by Guideposts
16 East 34th Street
New York, New York 10016
www.Guideposts.com

Distributed by Ideals Publications, a division of Guideposts
2636 Elm Hill Pike, Suite 120
Nashville, Tennessee 37214

Guideposts and *Ideals* are registered trademarks of Guideposts.

Acknowledgments
Every attempt has been made to credit the sources of copyrighted material used in this book. If any such acknowledgment has been inadvertently omitted or miscredited, receipt of such information would be appreciated.

Scripture quotations marked CEV are from the Contemporary English Version, copyright © 1995 by the American Bible Society. Used by permission.

Scripture quotations marked HCSB are from the Holman Christian Standard Bible®, copyright © 1999, 2000, 2002, 2003 by Holman Bible Publishers. Used by permission. Holman Christian Standard Bible®, Holman CSB®, and HCSB® are federally registered trademarks of Holman Bible Publishers.

Scripture quotations marked MSG are from *The Message*. Copyright © 1993, 1994, 1995, 1996, 2000, 2001, 2002. Used by permission of NavPress Publishing Group.

Scripture quotations marked NASB are from the New American Standard Bible®, copyright © 1960, 1962, 1963, 1968, 1971, 1973, 1975, 1977, 1995 by The Lockman Foundation. Used by permission.

Scripture quotations marked NIV are from the Holy Bible, New Inter national Version®. Copyright © 1973, 1978, 1984, International Bible Society. Used by permission of Zondervan Publishing House. All rights reserved.

Scripture quotations marked NKJV are taken from the New King James Version. Copyright © 1982 by Thomas Nelson, Inc. Used by permission. All rights reserved.

Scripture quotations marked NLT are from the *Holy Bible*, New Living Translation, copyright © 1996, 2004. Used by permission of Tyndale House Publishers, Inc., Wheaton, IL 60189. All rights reserved.

Library of Congress Cataloging-in-Publication Data

McAnally, Bryan.

  Life after death & heaven and hell / Bryan McAnally.

    p. cm. – (The indispensable guide to practically everything)

  ISBN 978-0-8249-4773-6

  1. Future life–Biblical teaching. 2. Future life–Christianity–Miscellanea. 3. Heaven–Biblical teaching. 4. Heaven–Christianity–Miscellanea. 5. Hell–Biblical teaching. 6. Hell–Christianity–Miscellanea. I. Title. II. Title: Life after death and heaven and hell.

  BS680.F83M36 2009

  236–dc22

                                    2009003910

Editor: Lila Empson
Cover and interior design: Whisner Design Group
Typesetting: Educational Publishing Concepts

Printed and bound in the United States of America

10 9 8 7 6 5 4 3 2

Take all the pleasures of all the spheres,
and multiply each through endless years—
one minute of heaven is worth them all.

Thomas Moore

Contents

Introduction 13

Death—The Beginning of the Next Life 17

1. The Inevitability of Physical Death 19
2. FAQ—What Happens to the Body at Death? 23
3. FAQ—What Happens to the Mind at Death? 25
4. FAQ—What Happens to the Spirit at Death? 27
5. FAQ—What Is the Purpose of Life? 29
6. FAQ—How Do I Live After I Die? 33
7. FAQ—What Does It Mean to Live Forever? 35

Final Judgment—The Decision That Determines Your Eternity 39

8. Meet the Judge—God 41
9. Meet Your Accuser—Satan 43
10. Meet Your Advocate—Jesus 45
11. The Basis of Judgment—Grace vs. Works 47
12. The Trial of Judgment—Standing Before God 51

13. FAQ—What Happens When the Verdict Is "Guilty!"? 55

14. FAQ—What Happens When the Verdict Is "Forgiven!"? 57

15. FAQ—What Are the Common Excuses That God Rejects? 59

16. FAQ—Are We Already in Heaven or Hell? 63

17. FAQ—What About Those Who Never Heard About Jesus? 67

18. FAQ—Is Purgatory Real? 71

19. FAQ—Are There Levels of Heaven and Hell? 73

20. FAQ—Does Everyone Get to Go to Heaven? 77

Heaven— Everybody's Hope and God's Promise to Welcome You Home

.... 79

21. God's Story of Eternity—Heaven Now and Heaven to Come 81

22. Perfection Realized—The Environment of Heaven 85

23. Watchless and Clockless—The Endlessness of Heaven 89

24. The Activities in Heaven—The Comings and Goings
    in Eternity 91

25. The Civilization of Heaven—Government and
    Community in Eternity 95

26. FAQ—Does Heaven *Really* Exist? 97

27. FAQ—Where Is Heaven Located? 99

28. FAQ—What Does It Mean to Praise God for Eternity? 101

29. FAQ—Is Saint Peter the Doorman of the Pearly Gates? 103

30. FAQ—Do All Babies Get to Go to Heaven? 105

31. FAQ—What Will We Eat and Drink in Heaven? 109

God—Describing the Indescribable
Host of Heaven 111

32. God in Heaven—The Fatherly King 113

33. Jesus in Heaven—The Heavenly Responsibilities of
    the Son of God 115

34. The Holy Spirit in Heaven—The Counseling
    Creator in Eternity 119

35. The Eternal Word of God—The Role of the Bible
    in Heaven 121

36. FAQ—What Will It Mean to See God in Heaven? 123

37. FAQ—How Will God Rule in Eternity? 125

38. FAQ—How Will God Relate to His Creation in Eternity? 127

39. FAQ—What Are the Names of God in Heaven? 131

Angels—God's Messengers 133

40. Instant Messaging, Invincible Military—
    The Responsibilities of Angels 137

41. The Named Angels—Meet God's Most Famous Messengers 139

42. Historic Angelic Battles and What You
Can Know from Them... 141

43. The Role of Fallen Angels in Temptation,
Possession, and Sin 143

44. FAQ—What Is the Role of Angels in a Person's Death? 147

45. FAQ—How Do You Relate to Angelic Beings in This Life? 149

46. FAQ—How Will You Relate to Angels in Eternity? 153

47. FAQ—Are Angels Really People with Wings? 155

48. FAQ—When Did God Create Angels? 159

49. FAQ—What Are the Limitations of Angels?............................. 163

Satan in the Afterlife

Satan in the Afterlife 165

50. The Origin of Satan.. 167

51. The Ambition of Satan 171

52. The Animosity of Satan.. 173

53. The Tactics of Satan.. 175

54. The Partners of Satan... 177

55. The Defeat of Satan 181

56. The Punishment of Satan.. 185

57. FAQ—Is Satan Really Real? 187

58. FAQ—What Are Satan's Limitations?.................................. 189

Hell—Real, Hot, and Hopeless 191

59. The Reality of Hell 193

60. The Isolation of Hell 195

61. The Endlessness of Hell 197

62. FAQ—When Did God Create Hell? 199

63. FAQ—Why Did God Create Hell? 201

64. FAQ—Who Is in Hell? 203

65. FAQ—Is Hell a Literal Lake of Fire? 207

66. FAQ—Who Is the Overseer of Hell? 211

You in the Afterlife 215

67. Your Body in the Afterlife 217

68. Your Home in the Afterlife 221

69. Your Work in the Afterlife 223

70. Your Relationships in the Afterlife 225

71. Your Past and the Afterlife 229

72. Your Rewards in the Afterlife 231

73. Your Attitude in the Afterlife 235

74. FAQ—Will the Physical Effects of This Life
    Be Evident in Eternity? 237

75. FAQ—Will I Mourn Loved Ones Not in Heaven? 239

76. FAQ—Will I Recognize Friends and Family in Heaven? 243

77. FAQ—Will My Marriage and Family Relationships
    Continue in Heaven? 245

78. FAQ—Will I Be Able to Ask God Questions? 247

79. FAQ—Will My Pets Be in Heaven? 249

80. FAQ—Will Heaven Be Boring? 251

The truest end of life is to know the life that never ends.

William Penn

Introduction

*Looking for God—or Heaven—by exploring space is like
reading or seeing all Shakespeare's plays in the hope
that you will find Shakespeare as one of the characters.*

C. S. Lewis

In those words, Lewis acknowledged humanity's timeless search for answers to the question of what happens to a person when the current life ends. Scientists, scribes, scholars, and seekers have contributed theories, myths, ideas, and opinions throughout every age and generation. While the answers to these questions are stitched into the fabric of reality, nowhere are the answers more apparent than in the words recorded in the Bible.

The revelation offered in the Bible regarding heaven, hell, and the afterlife suggests that God does not want humans to be ignorant about these matters. While much has been misunderstood, misreported, or altogether distorted throughout time, the

> We are looking forward to the new heavens and new earth he has promised, a world filled with God's righteousness. And so, dear friends, while you are waiting for these things to happen, make every effort to be found living peaceful lives that are pure and blameless in his sight.
>
> 2 Peter 3:13–14 NLT

Bible offers an unchanged, reliable record that addresses important aspects of this temporary present life as well as of the unending one that will follow. God wants every person to know about him. He desires that every person be informed about the nature of this life and the next. He wants every person to be aware of heaven, of hell, of angels and demons, and especially of Jesus.

> Any one who feels the full significance of what is involved in knowing the truth has a coercive feeling that Eternity has been set within us, that our finite life is deeply rooted in the all-pervading Infinite.
>
> Rufus M. Jones

Remarkably, God is not content merely to alert people to the reality of the afterlife. He has packaged his revelation to humans in an exquisite invitation that he offers to every person so that each one may respond to it. It is impossible to separate what the Bible says about the afterlife from what God invites every person to experience. God offers his best for the afterlife. It is God's intent to make people aware of heaven and hell so that every person would opt for heaven, reject hell, and agree to follow God's flawless path. While full understanding about the afterlife can be attained only when the current life ends, a comprehensive appreciation about it is available now to everyone who earnestly seeks it.

To go to heaven, fully to enjoy God, is infinitely better than the most pleasant accommodations here.

Jonathan Edwards

Remember your leaders who have spoken God's word to you. As you carefully observe the outcome of their lives, imitate their faith.

Hebrews 13:7 HCSB

"The new heavens and the new earth which I make
will endure before Me," declares the LORD.

Isaiah 66:22 NASB

Death—The Beginning of the Next Life

Every person approaches the unavoidable, unknown date at the end of physical life. Then, when everlasting life begins immediately thereafter, all life's questions are answered, and faith will be proven either flawed or fulfilled.

Contents

The Inevitability of Physical Death..................................... 19

FAQ—What Happens to the Body at Death?...................... 23

FAQ—What Happens to the Mind at Death? 25

FAQ—What Happens to the Spirit at Death? 27

FAQ—What Is the Purpose of Life?.................................... 29

FAQ—How Do I Live After I Die? 33

FAQ—What Does It Mean to Live Forever? 35

The last enemy to be destroyed is death.

1 Corinthians 15:26 NIV

The Inevitability of Physical Death

Why do people have to die? Most people are searching for answers to what will happen to them after death, because nobody lives forever. Death happens, and there is no escaping its inevitability. People of all ages and all social backgrounds die. It doesn't matter how much money they have or how health-conscious they are. Despite the fact that death is unavoidable, however, physical death is *not* the final chapter of life. Death is, in fact, a new beginning.

✴

People were not created to die. Originally, God created humans to live forever with him in paradise. God made all of creation for their pleasure and benefit. Adam and Eve were designed to fill the earth with their descendants. People were God's ultimate, special creation that would rule the earth in perfect harmony with him as their Creator.

Even before he created the universe and everything in it, however, God knew that his ideal arrangement would be challenged. The story is familiar: God gave Adam and Eve a whole garden full of trees. They could eat the fruit of any of them, except one. God told them that if they ate the fruit from that one tree, they would die. God warned them. But God knew that Satan would tempt Adam and Eve to distrust God and eat the fruit.

The Lord God commanded the man, "You are free to eat from any tree in the garden; but you must not eat from the tree of the knowledge of good and evil, for when you eat of it you will surely die."

Genesis 2:16–17 NIV

No one can live forever; all will die. No one can escape the power of the grave.

Psalm 89:48 NLT

Adam and Eve fell for Satan's wiles despite God's clear warnings and exhortations. They didn't believe God's warning. How could eating fruit kill them? They believed Satan and in so doing turned from God. God cursed both Satan and the earth for their respective roles in the rebellion, but God showed his mercy to Adam and Eve in a way that at first read seems unfair: He sentenced them to death.

How could a death sentence be God's most merciful act? If God had allowed Adam and Eve to live forever—as God had originally wanted—they would have lived forever, yes, but separated from him. God knew this would happen, though, and he had already prepared a solution. Because Adam and Eve's mutiny required a death sentence, God had designed a loophole. Yes, they would have to die physically. But they could be reconciled with God and live with him forever spiritually!

To do that, Adam and Eve needed faith. That was the fix. God made faith the requirement for every person seeking him—faith could fix what human disobedience breaks.

With Adam and Eve's rebellion, disobedience to God became part of the human condition, passed on in endless progression from human to human. Every person is born with rebellion against God. Accordingly, every person has to face death. Thanks to God's loophole, however, every person has the opportunity to be reconciled with God and to live with him forever.

In the earliest generations after Adam and Eve, each death was a reminder of the consequence of the broken relationship between God and humans. People could still remember that the now terminal human life had once been endless.

Yet as generations passed and populations expanded, people forgot why they died. The whole meaning of death was lost. People invented stories to bring nobility and significance to death. When people forgot the real reason why they had to die, they created myths about death. They created a profusion of gods and goddesses and mythological warriors who supposedly ushered the living to the dead. They developed ceremonies and rituals and tried to keep connections with their loved ones who had died.

Death is a fascinating mystery. Scientists study death in inconclusive attempts to capture what happens when a person dies. Philosophers ponder the meaning of life in the context of death. Artists strive to give meaning to death through paintings, sculptures, words, and songs. Rulers attempt to delay, deny, or otherwise avoid death altogether. Yet despite all these efforts, death always has its due. People keep dying at the rate of 100 percent. Science cannot stop it, predict it, or explain it. Faith, however, promises that when your physical life ends, your afterlife begins.

> What a miserable person I am. Who will rescue me from this body that is doomed to die?
>
> Romans 7:24 CEV

Digging Deeper

The Bible records a fascinating account of a man named Lazarus who was resurrected from the dead by the command of Jesus (John 11). Lazarus had become ill. When he died, his sisters wrapped him in burial cloths and sealed him in a tomb. The Bible even notes that Lazarus's body had begun to decompose. When Jesus arrived four days later, he wept over the death of his friend Lazarus before he raised him back to life. In mourning Lazarus, Jesus demonstrated that death is a real, significant event that even he found troubling.

Points to Remember

- Originally, you were created to live eternally. You were created to live forever with God in a perfect, earthly paradise.

- Death is the consequence of disobedience to God, a consequence that was passed along to you before you were born.

- God's mercy allows you the opportunity to be reunited with God through faith.

- Everybody dies. Nobody escapes death. It is important to understand death so that you can understand God's plan for eternal life.

Check Your Understanding

▪ Why were humans created?

God created people in his image to live with him forever in the earthly paradise called Eden. They and their descendants were to have enjoyed the fullness of God's creation and lived in harmony with God eternally.

▪ Why do all humans have to face death?

Every human faces death because every human is born to rebel against God. Death is not just the consequence of the first rebellion of Adam and Eve; death is the consequence of every rebellious act of disobedience by every person who has ever lived.

▪ Why is death a consequence of but not a punishment for human rebellion?

Death is a consequence but not a punishment because death became the necessary event for a person's restoration to God. Because of the redemptive purpose of death, it is incorrect to view it as punishment.

FAQ—What Happens to the Body at Death?

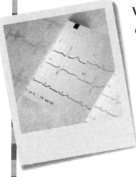

When you are breathing your last, a series of physical events take place in quick succession. These events signal the end of your life on earth and the onset of death. Regardless of age, race, economic or social status, or religion, you will experience these common phenomena: essential body functions—activity in your heart and your brain—cease, and the result is death, the end of physical life.

Regardless of the official cause of death, what causes you to stop living is the lack of oxygen being supplied to the cells. Blood, which transports oxygen to the cells as nourishment and escorts carbon dioxide to be expelled from the body, stops circulating. When this happens, the lungs stop breathing and the heart stops beating. The body cannot live without oxygenated cells.

Because of advances in medical technology, breathing and circulation can sometimes be performed artificially for a person who would otherwise be unable to perform these functions independently. Because of this, another marker of

It's better to go to a funeral than to attend a feast; funerals remind us that we all must die.

Ecclesiastes 7:2 CEV

David, after serving his own generation in God's plan, fell asleep, was buried with his fathers, and decayed.

Acts 13:36 HCSB

physical death is the end of electrical activity in the brain, as monitored by trained physicians. This also is caused by lack of oxygen. Brain death occurs when the cerebral neurons die due to a lack of blood flow and oxygen. Brain death is irreversible.

When a body dies, natural processes begin. *Livor mortis*—the pooling of the reserves of blood in the lowest elevated parts of the body—sets in first. Then the body begins to stiffen in a process known as *rigor mortis*. It is a myth that hair and fingernails and toenails continue to grow after death. All cells begin a natural process of decomposition. Eventually the entire body decomposes, leaving behind scant skeletal remains as most of the person's physical body disintegrates in accord with the burial environment.

Points to Remember

- Death is defined by the stoppage of blood circulation, breathing, or brain activity.
- At death, life functions cease and decomposition begins. Physical decomposition depends upon the conditions of the environment into which the body is placed permanently.
- Physical death and bodily decomposition can be delayed or interrupted, but never avoided.

Check Your Understanding

- **What is *livor mortis* and why is it significant?**

Livor mortis is a post-death physical process where the reserves of a person's blood settle in the lowest elevated part of the body. It is significant because it is evidence of the termination of blood flow at the end of life.

- **How is death defined in medical terms?**

Death is defined as the cessation of cardiac activity, the cessation of breathing, or the absence of electrical brain activity.

FAQ—What Happens to the Mind at Death?

Observing a physical body is simple, and because of this there is near unanimous agreement about what happens to a body when physical death occurs. It is impossible, however, to observe the human mind comprehensively, and there is widespread disagreement about what happens to the mind upon physical death. The opinions of science are inconclusive, philosophies are debatable, and world religions are divided over this matter. Even so, the Bible teaches that mind and soul are eternally connected to the spirit; whatever happens to a person's spirit also happens to the person's mind and soul.

Understanding common and unique terms helps explain what happens to the mind and soul at death:

Brain. The brain is the physical human organ of cognitive processes such as thoughts, feelings, emotions, attitudes, and behaviors.

Mind. The mind is a function of the brain and is where consciousness dwells (expressed in the actions of comprehending, perceiving, evaluating, processing, and acting). The mind offers a person self-awareness and a sense of perspective within existence.

He restores my soul, He guides me in the paths of righteousness for His name's sake.

Psalm 23:3 NKJV

The LORD redeems the soul of His servants.

Psalm 34:22 NASB

Soul. The soul is a theological concept. It is the living conscience distinct from but interworking with the physical body. In Christianity, the mind and the soul are synonymous, where comprehension, perception, evaluation, process, and action dwell alongside intellect, discernment, and judgment along with lusts, passions, and cravings. The soul/mind is the bridge between the body and the spirit.

Spirit. The spirit is a theological concept. The eternal essence of an individual is unique to the person.

From a scientific standpoint, physical death also means the death of the mind, because the mind is merely a complex function of the brain. However, Christianity teaches that the soul/mind bridges the body and the spirit.

The Old Testament perspective was that when a person physically died, his soul/mind "slept" in a state of unconsciousness in a place called *Sheol,* which meant "the grave." However, Christianity teaches that death affects only the physical body and that when a person experiences physical death, his soul/mind and his spirit continue to live.

Points to Remember

- From a biblical perspective, the soul is the same as the mind, but it is distinct from the body and from the spirit. The soul/mind is the cognitive bridge between the body and the spirit.

  - When a person's body dies, his soul continues to live along with his spirit. What awaits the spirit beyond death also awaits the mind/soul.

Check Your Understanding

- **What is the function of the mind, and what is its relationship to the body and the spirit?**

The mind perceives, comprehends, and discerns. It compels the body toward action. It acts as a "bridge" between the body and the spirit.

- **Why is it important to understand that the mind/soul lives beyond death along with the spirit?**

It is important to know that the mind/soul lives beyond death along with the spirit because this means that what is unique about a person remains alive after physical death.

FAQ—What Happens to the Spirit at Death?

The concept of the human spirit tends to be an idea reserved for theological considerations. Science has no comment on whether or not the spirit exists, much less what happens to the spirit following death. However, the Bible clearly teaches that every person is born with a spirit. The spirit is what distinguishes humans as created uniquely in the image of God. Furthermore, biblical teachings reveal that a person's spirit is created to live forever. When the physical body dies, the spirit continues and begins its eternal experience.

When God created humans, he breathed into them the spirit of life. The spirit is a person's individual and eternal essence that continues to live after physical death. Prior to their rebellion against God, Adam and Eve were created to live with God forever in soul/mind, body, and spirit. Their spirits were in union with God's own Spirit. Their rebellion betrayed their natural spiritual connection to God, however, and veiled the soul/mind's ability to perceive God and relate to him experientially.

This disconnection with God necessitated the consequence of physical death. Through physical death, God can restore a person's soul/mind and spirit to a right, eternal relationship with him.

May God himself, the God who makes everything holy and whole, make you holy and whole, put you together—spirit, soul, and body—and keep you fit for the coming of our Master, Jesus Christ.

1 Thessalonians 5:23 MSG

The man without the Spirit does not accept the things that come from the Spirit of God.

1 Corinthians 2:14 NIV

At death, a person passes from the terminal physical life to an eternal spiritual life. The person continues to live as a unique individual in soul/mind and spirit. The person is still individual and whole, but without the body that housed the soul/mind and spirit for the person's physical life.

Jesus taught that the most important concern for anyone was what happens to his soul/mind and spirit following death. Jesus taught that the body dies and decays but that the spirit lives forever. He taught people to understand God's plan to restore the eternal relationship that continues after death. Jesus taught that God did not want even one person to physically die without first receiving God's spiritual reconciliation.

Points to Remember

- God breathed the spirit of life into humans as eternal beings and as an expression of creating them in his own image.

- Though the physical body inevitably dies, the spiritual being inevitably lives. Jesus taught that the most important thing a person could do while physically living is to prepare for the eternal spiritual life that follows death.

Check Your Understanding

- **What is the spirit of a person?**

The spirit of a person is the unique "breath of life" given by God to each individual. This breath of life is the innermost part of a person's being. Along with the mind/soul, a person's spirit lives beyond death.

- **Why does it matter that every person's spirit will have a face-to-face encounter with God?**

After death, every person will have a personal meeting with God. This meeting is significant because this meeting reveals the determination of where the person will exist eternally.

FAQ—What Is the Purpose of Life?

Every person is created in the three-part image of God. Just as God is Father, Son, and Holy Spirit, every person is body, mind, and spirit. Even before the creation of the universe, God knew that the original rebellion of Adam and Eve would corrupt his union with humans. Therefore, the Father, in an incomprehensible expression of love, sent Jesus into time to reconcile the broken relationship with humans. As a result, every human has the opportunity to receive God's reconciliation and enjoy a reunified relationship with God as he originally intended.

Immediately after the disobedience of Adam and Eve, God revealed his plan to reconcile all people. God told Adam and Eve that one day a descendant of theirs would be born who would fix what they had broken and that all people of all time could experience the benefit of his work.

God faithfully repeated this promise throughout history, protecting and preserving Adam and Eve's descendants. God revealed himself to a particular descendant named Abraham, promising that one day Abraham's descendants would bless the entire world. This revelation caused Abraham to live in obedience to God, and God orchestrated global events to prepare the welcome of the special person appointed for this special purpose.

In time, the special person promised by God became known by the title *Messiah*, a Hebrew word meaning,

You will be saved, if you honestly say, "Jesus is Lord," and if you believe with all your heart that God raised him from death.

Romans 10:9 CEV

My purpose in writing is simply this: that you who believe in God's Son will know beyond the shadow of a doubt that you have eternal life, the reality and not the illusion.

1 John 5:13 MSG

"anointed one." As generations descended from Abraham, God used prophets to reveal more about the Messiah's identity: where he would be born, to which branch of Abraham's family, and what he would do. The revelations were amazing: he would perform miracles, he would be a prophet, priest, and king, and he would rule for one thousand years.

As incredible as these predictions may have been, there were others that were practically inconceivable: the Messiah would be God in the flesh, he would be rejected by his people and killed, he would lie dead for three days, and he would then be resurrected.

Two thousand years ago, a man named Jesus was born in Bethlehem under miraculous circumstances to a virgin named Mary. Jesus grew to manhood and began spreading the message of the soon-coming kingdom of God. He invited people to follow him. He made claims of knowing the mind of God, calling him his "Father." Jesus performed many miracles, declaring that he did so only to demonstrate his power to do the even greater work of forgiving a person's offenses against God. Opposing religious leaders labeled him a blasphemer and attributed his miracles to Satan.

Jesus raised the dead from the grave and predicted his own death, burial, and resurrection. Within three years of when he first started, Jesus was indeed crucified for blasphemy and was buried. Many of the details of his arrest, torture, death, and burial occurred exactly according to prophecies recorded hundreds of years earlier.

Friends buried Jesus in a borrowed garden tomb protected by a large stone and guarded by Roman soldiers. Three days later, his tomb was found open, and Jesus' body was missing. That same day, Jesus was seen among his followers, fully alive and interacting with them. Jesus dwelt among them for forty days, viewed by more than five hundred witnesses. Jesus told his followers that God freely offered forgiveness to anyone who asked and that God's forgiveness gave the gift of heaven and eternal life. Jesus commanded his followers to take this message to the entire world.

More than two thousand years later, billions of people have come to understand that Jesus is God's promised Messiah. He rose from the dead and went to heaven while alive. Because of this, people in every generation from virtually every culture have come to believe that Jesus is God, the Lord over creation. They believe that their hope for heaven is found in accepting the biblical promise that Jesus died on the cross so that every person can live.

> I call heaven and earth as witnesses against you today that I have set before you life and death, blessing and curse. Choose life so that you and your descendants may live.
>
> Deuteronomy 30:19 HCSB

God's offer of forgiveness and heaven must be accepted while a person is still physically alive. All people are born spiritually separated from God because of their own rebellion against him. God invites every person to make a conscientious decision to trust God and believe in the truth of Jesus. Those who do so will reunite with God in mind and spirit and will be with God in heaven forever after their physical lives end.

Myth Buster

Many modern thinkers suggest Jesus never claimed to be God, that he merely offered an example of how to live and to encourage people to love one another. While Jesus did tell people to love one another and was the best example of moral living, he would not have had to die on a cross to be this message and example. Jesus was killed exactly because he claimed  to be able to forgive man's offenses against God. This was an ability believed to be reserved for God alone. Jesus proved his identity when he rose from the grave three days later.

Points to Remember

- God planned to repair the broken relationship with humans by forgiving their offenses. He promised that he would send them a Messiah who would give them this gift.

    - Jesus was the fulfillment of God's promise. Jesus said that anyone who believed his message would receive God's forgiveness.

- God's offer of forgiveness through belief in Jesus is freely available, but the decision to believe must be made while physically living.

Check Your Understanding

- **Why does it matter that God knew that humans would rebel against him before he began creation?**

God's prior knowledge of human rebellion demonstrates God's vast love to go ahead with creation and to provide a solution to reconcile people back to him.

- **Why is it significant that Jesus fulfilled prophecies about the Messiah?**

Jesus' fulfillment of prophecy demonstrated that he is God's Messiah. God wanted people to recognize the one who was especially suited to overcome humanity's rebellion problem and to put their faith in him to do that which they could not do themselves.

- **Why does a person have to believe that Jesus is God to be forgiven?**

God provided the only way to fix people's broken relationship with him when he sent Jesus as he had promised. Believing that Jesus is God provides people with God's forgiveness and gives them the gift of heaven.

FAQ—How Do I Live After I Die?

Death is recognized as "the end" because every physical function of the body stops. Breathing, brain activity, and the heart all stop. At death, the body immediately transitions from growth and maintenance to decay and destruction. Ironically, it is only when the temporary physical life ends that the eternal spiritual life begins. Faith-based concepts, ideas, and personalities instantly become absolute, clear realities at the onset of spiritual life after physical death.

The apostle Paul described the physical body as a "body of death." This means that the body is limited in what it can do, and the individual is limited in what he can do with it. The physical body constrains and restrains the mind and the spirit. Most important, the physical body is destined to die. The mind and the spirit—restricted by physical limitations, urges, and temptations—struggle to comprehend spiritual realities as long as the physical body lives.

At death, the mind and the spirit are immediately unbound from the physical body. A person then exists solely in the spiritual reality of the afterlife. The need for faith ends at the point of death. All matters believed by faith prior to death will be revealed. Faith is trust in something that cannot be proven. Faith is required while in the physical body on earth because the basis of belief cannot be established objectively; people's belief in God comes from their confidence that he is indeed the Creator of all things and the lover of humankind. Opinions

He has made everything appropriate in its time. He has also put eternity in their hearts, but man cannot discover the work God has done from beginning to end.

Ecclesiastes 3:11 HCSB

Your throne, O LORD, has stood from time immemorial. You yourself are from the everlasting past.

Psalm 93:2 NLT

on spiritual matters will be affirmed or refuted after physical death, and every person will immediately understand God as he truly is.

Your physical body is merely the container for your spirit. Neither time nor space will constrain your spirit after your body dies. Your spirit will enjoy everlasting life.

Points to Remember

- Eternity is life outside time. While eternity itself has no beginning, you will experience your beginning in eternity at the exact moment of physical death.

  - Faith and belief are out of date in eternity. Things are *believed in* in the physical life, but either *are* or *are not* in eternity. The hopes of the physical life are either disproven or fulfilled in the reality of the spiritual life.

Check Your Understanding

- **What does it mean that humans are created for eternity?**

People's lives are marked by physical death of the body, but this death does not mark the end of the mind and the spirit. Those aspects live forever.

- **Why is faith important in physical life if there is no faith in the spiritual afterlife?**

Faith is essential in the physical life because it establishes the destination for the person's mind and spirit in the eternal life that follows. Faith decisions made while living on earth will certainly determine what happens to a person at the instantaneous onset of eternity following physical death.

FAQ—What Does It Mean to Live Forever?

At various places within its pages, the Bible describes with dramatic imagery the brevity of life in the context of time. Life is described as withering grass, as a vanishing mist, as water spilled on the ground that cannot be recovered, and as a fleeting shadow. By comparison, the Bible describes God as the Ancient of Days, the everlasting Lord, and the eternal King. Passing from physical death to spiritual life means moving from within time to beyond time.

✳

Virtually every tombstone confirms the fact that humans are all born limited in earthly time: John Doe, 1900–1999, R.I.P. Time limits human understanding of God. Time inhibits our human ability to comprehend what existence is like outside it. The Bible reveals that God existed before time, operates completely apart from time, and will reign after time has ended because God's purpose for time will have ended as well. There is no need for time in eternity.

God is the Creator who has no beginning or end. He existed before the words "in the beginning" revealed in Genesis 1:1. He is ever-present and omnipresent. Jesus described himself as "the First and the Last,

You have made known to me the path of life; you will fill me with joy in your presence, with eternal pleasures at your right hand.

Psalm 16:11 NIV

The mercy of the LORD is from everlasting to everlasting on those who fear Him, and His righteousness to children's children.

Psalm 103:17 NKJV

the Beginning and the End," meaning that all existence is contained within God's provision and that nothing exists outside it.

Time is perhaps best understood as God's resource. Prior to the rebellion of Adam and Eve, God had no need for time because humans were created to live with him in unity forever. Yet God saw beforehand that they would disobey him, so he instituted creation within the construct of time. This tool of time would also much later include an experience where God would leave heaven and himself pay the penalty for the wrongdoings of all people. God's plan also included the yet-to-come conclusion of time. With this conclusion, perfect existence would continue as the fullness of God's plan, and time was no longer necessary.

Until the arrival of the end of earthly time, people continue to pass from time-bound physical life to never-ending spiritual life. As we die, God

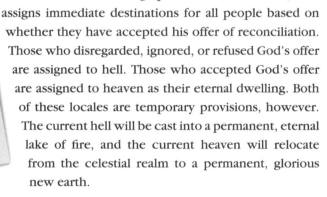

assigns immediate destinations for all people based on whether they have accepted his offer of reconciliation. Those who disregarded, ignored, or refused God's offer are assigned to hell. Those who accepted God's offer are assigned to heaven as their eternal dwelling. Both of these locales are temporary provisions, however. The current hell will be cast into a permanent, eternal lake of fire, and the current heaven will relocate from the celestial realm to a permanent, glorious new earth.

Theologians disagree about whether time will cease altogether or continue after God's plan for redemption ends and eternity begins. Some suggest that time itself will end and that heaven will be forever understood as a perpetual of state of living in the present, forever unfolding without end. Other scholars reason that time will continue to exist but that it will be redeemed and expressed in perfection.

Heaven and hell are the two ultimate destinations for human souls. We humans are finite beings. Accordingly, it is unlikely that finite people, whether in heaven or hell, will be able to be in multiple places the way infinite God is able to be everywhere at one time. Similarly, it is unlikely that humans will be able to go instantly to different locations. This suggests that time in some form may exist after death but that it is a mystery how humans will operate within it.

Existence beyond this physical life is a reality that does not have an end. For the person who will be with God forever, it means that this perfect union will never end. For the person who will be separated from God

> Jesus Christ is the same yesterday, today, and forever. So do not be attracted by strange, new ideas. Your strength comes from God's grace.
>
> Hebrews 13:8–9 NLT

forever, it means that there is no longer any hope for pardon. When a person passes from the physical life to the eternal life his existence in that realm of sorrow or joy is final and everlasting. Understanding this, the opportunity of heaven that God offers to all people during the physical life is even more remarkable.

Digging Deeper

Time is a special dimension of physical reality. Humans can move freely within space—forward, backward, up, down, left, or right. Human movement within time, however, is limited. We cannot go back in time, nor can we remain in a single moment. Time continually moves forward. When life ends, every person faces his spirit's eternal destination—"Each person is destined to die once and after that comes judgment" (Hebrews 9:27 NLT). It makes sense to accept God's offer of heaven that he makes to every living person.

Points to Remember

- Theologians disagree about whether *eternity* means "time forevermore" or "time nevermore." However, the consensus of eternity is the promise of a future that has no end.

- When a person passes from the present physical life, he immediately begins his eternal life in an unalterable destination. He will be either in the presence of God or apart from God.

Check Your Understanding

■ **What is the current purpose of time?**

Time is God's tool to move humanity through the progression of his plan for creation. He used time to provide a way for Jesus to enter this world as a human in order to die for our offenses.

■ **Why is time important to every person living in the physical realm?**

Time in the physical realm is important because it is within time that a person has the opportunity to respond to God's offer of heaven. Anyone who accepts this offer will experience eternity in heaven.

■ **What will eternity look like?**

While the specific understanding of eternity is elusive, it is understood to mean that it is an unchangeable future without end. Whether a person begins the eternal existence in hell or in heaven, he remains there forever.

■ **What is God's relationship with time?**

God existed before time, operates completely apart from time, and will reign after time has ended because God's purpose for time will have ended as well. There is no need for time in eternity.

Final Judgment—The Decision That Determines Your Eternity

Every person faces two judgments after physical life ends. Once for their faith, and later for their life's efforts. God wants everyone to know that the physical life matters and determines a person's eternal destination.

Contents

Meet the Judge—God 41

Meet Your Accuser—Satan 43

Meet Your Advocate—Jesus 45

The Basis of Judgment—Grace vs. Works 47

The Trial of Judgment—Standing Before God 51

FAQ—What Happens When the Verdict Is "Guilty!"? 55

FAQ—What Happens When the Verdict Is "Forgiven!"? 57

FAQ—What Are the Common Excuses That God Rejects? 59

FAQ—Are We Already in Heaven or Hell? 63

FAQ—What About Those Who Never Heard About Jesus? 67

FAQ—Is Purgatory Real? 71

FAQ—Are There Levels of Heaven and Hell? 73

FAQ—Does Everyone Get to Go to Heaven? 77

The LORD shall endure forever; He has prepared His throne for judgment.

Psalm 9:7 NKJV

Meet the Judge—God

One of God's unchanging characteristics is that he is guided by fairness. This means that he is impartial and unprejudiced. God determined that all of us would pass from this physical life to our eternal destination based upon God's justice. God judges each person individually and without favoritism. God evaluates the evidence based on fair criteria and renders the verdict.

From the beginning of time, God has judged his creation, that is, God has made decisions with authority. On each day of the six days of creation, he judged his work "good." When God created humans, he judged them "very good." After Adam and Eve disobeyed, God's judgment banned them from Paradise, sentenced them to labor and strife, and cursed Satan and the earth. God judged humanity at the time of Noah and flooded the earth. God judged the evil cities of Sodom and Gomorrah and sent fiery hail upon them. The New Testament declares God to be the Judge of all people and all nations.

God's judgment is marked by goodness and fairness. It is without mercy—that is, there are no exceptions to God's judgment, and no one can argue against it. God's judgment will overrule any objections. In fact, the Bible says that anyone who stands in judgment according to the law will be silenced from objections by the overwhelming evidence against them.

> According to my gospel, God will judge the secrets of men through Christ Jesus.
>
> Romans 2:16 NASB
>
> When all has been heard, the conclusion of the matter is: fear God and keep His commands, because this is for all humanity. For God will bring every act to judgment, including every hidden thing, whether good or evil.
>
> Ecclesiastes 12:13–14 HCSB

God's standard for judgment is holiness, and each person will be measured without favoritism to that standard. While even one shortcoming is enough to disqualify a person from God's reward, God's plan offers hope for everyone who accepts it. God is happy with any person who believes in Jesus and follows his teachings. God forgives those people of their shortcomings, and he marks them as holy. To them he gives heaven and blessing.

Points to Remember

- God has judged individuals, nations, and creation itself from the dawn of time.

- God's judgment is based on his standard of holiness.

- God's judgment is always perfect.

- God's judgment is without mercy.

- God's judgment will either vindicate or condemn the judged.

Check Your Understanding

- **What does it mean that God's standard for judgment is his own holiness?**

For God's standard for judgment to be his own holiness means that each person being judged will be compared to God's standard of sinless perfection. Anyone who does not reach that standard will be found guilty.

- **Why is it important that God's judgment is merciless?**

It is important to know that God's judgment is merciless because it reveals that God's standard is absolute and consistent. He will not change his judgment based upon anything other than the evidence presented before him.

Meet Your Accuser—Satan

The Bible paints the picture of a courtroom drama awaiting every person at the onset of eternal life. God alone is the Judge, because no one can exonerate himself. There is no jury to be swayed by public opinion or convincing excuses. However, this "court" has a formidable opponent. In addition to the Judge and the judged is an accuser. This accuser is known for his vicious attacks against goodness and righteousness. This accuser is Satan.

✳

The word *Satan* means "adversary," which speaks to the oppositional nature of the fallen angel Lucifer. He rebelled against God, and he hates humans as God's finest creation. Throughout history, Satan has connived to derail God's plan for humans. He plots and schemes, using powerful men and demonic power to bring chaos upon the earth. He operates in the dark arts of temptation, bribery, and deception, often with great degrees of temporary success.

Satan is never too busy to accuse an individual before God. Satan's goal is to kill people and destroy lives. Satan delights in accusing a person of evil. He relishes his role as accuser, and he faithfully fulfills his responsibilities to bring false as well as true charges against every person.

> Joshua the high priest was standing in front of the LORD's angel. And there was Satan, standing at Joshua's right side, ready to accuse him.
>
> Zechariah 3:1 CEV
>
> Satan, the one who deceives the whole world . . . the accuser of our brothers has been thrown out: the one who accuses them before our God day and night.
>
> Revelation 12:9–10 HCSB

Satan's tactics are time-tested. He artfully weaves lies among truths. His assault is a campaign to destroy the accused. God sees through the lies. However, if there is truth in the accusations, God sees that as well. Satan gleefully rejoices if the true evidence convicts the person and God's judgment casts him into hell.

Nevertheless, know this. The person's destruction is not Satan's true objective. Satan's accusations are not truly against the person; they are against God. Satan desires to overthrow God. Satan's tireless accusations against people are part of his evil, rebellious effort to defeat his Creator.

Points to Remember

- Satan hates every person. He is not trying to win converts. He is trying to destroy God's creation.

- Satan's goal is to bring lives to ruin.

- Satan accuses people using a mixture of true and false allegations in an attempt to destroy the individual.

- Satan's accusations are truly against God.

Check Your Understanding

- **What does it mean that Satan is "the accuser"?**

Satan's title "the accuser" means that Satan makes accusations to God against the individual in an attempt to force God to banish a person to hell.

- **What does it mean that Satan's ultimate objective is overthrowing God?**

For Satan, humans are a mere tool to be used in his rebellion against God. He strives to accuse people as a way to bring accusation against God. Satan's desire is to overthrow God and to reign as creation's king himself.

Meet Your Advocate—Jesus

During our physical lives, all of us will inevitably err in some manner that sufficiently disqualifies us from the right to be with God forever. Upon death, we will face legal proceedings where God renders judgment. Most of us will have no defense to the accusations levied against us by Satan. God foresaw this problem, however, and he devised the solution before he inaugurated creation. God already decided that he, not we, would bear the punishment for humanity's offenses. In doing so, he would be the perfect "courtroom advocate" for those of us who, while living the physical life, believe that Jesus is Lord.

Jesus was born without sin. At the same time he was fully God, he was also fully human, subject to human temptations. Yet he lived as he was born, sinless. God stepped out of the heavenly realm and lived a perfect life as a physical human named Jesus.

God used people's circumstances and prophets throughout the generations to communicate that Jesus would one day be born, live the perfect life without offending God's holiness, and die for the offenses of all the people. God promised that all who believe that Jesus is Lord would have their offenses attributed to Jesus. He would bear the guilt and the penalty for the sins of humanity. In this regard, Jesus would be the Advocate for those who believe in him.

> He took the punishment, and that made us whole. Through his bruises we get healed. We're all like sheep who've wandered off and gotten lost. We've all done our own thing, gone our own way. And GOD has piled all our sins, everything we've done wrong, on him, on him.
>
> Isaiah 53:5–6 MSG

> If anyone sins, we have an Advocate with the Father, Jesus Christ the righteous. And He Himself is the propitiation for our sins, and not for ours only but also for the whole world.
>
> 1 John 2:1–2 NKJV

Points to Remember

- Jesus was born into a human body.

- Jesus is God, and he is also God's Son. He determined to bear the punishment for people's offenses. His successful advocacy allows us to be judged worthy to enter heaven.

- All that is required to live forever with God is to believe during this physical life that Jesus is Lord.

Check Your Understanding

- **What does it mean that Jesus is our Advocate?**

Jesus' role as Advocate means that he will speak in defense of every person who believes in him as Lord. He sufficiently satisfied God's requirement that all offenses be judged, and this provides us with access to heaven forever.

- **What does it mean that a person's offenses are attributed to Jesus?**

When a person's offenses are attributed to Jesus, it means that rather than the person being held responsible for the consequences of their offenses against God, Jesus himself bears the consequences.

The Basis of Judgment—Grace vs. Works

The judgment of God is a serious matter that has caused people of every nation throughout history to strive to please God. The hope is that when they stand before God, their efforts will have earned his favor, granting them entrance into heaven. This perception is common, but mistaken. The Bible teaches that God judges by a different standard. He doesn't look at the things that impress people. Instead, he evaluates whether a person has accepted the offer he gives through Jesus. Humanity's way is works, but God's plan is grace.

Works is the concept that a person can do enough good things, or can stay away from enough bad things, to please God. This notion of human effort has been around from the earliest days. Ever since the time of Adam's son Cain, people have tried to please God through their efforts, either by "doing good" or by refraining from "doing bad." Often, these efforts are rooted in a baseless notion that God judges life based on a set of cosmic scales.

These efforts are expressed in many ways. Some people believe that God monitors church attendance, crediting people for regularly showing up in their congregation. They believe that if they give money to their church or to other charitable causes, then God marks their donations in a celestial ledger, tracking their benevolent offering in order to "pay off" penalties for other mistakes. In addition, some people think that volunteering at church or in the community will give them bonus points with God and perhaps

It is by grace you have been saved, through faith—and this not from yourselves, it is the gift of God—not by works, so that no one can boast.

Ephesians 2:8–9 NIV

We are all infected and impure with sin. When we display our righteous deeds, they are nothing but filthy rags.

Isaiah 64:6 NLT

cancel out some of their less-charitable activities. Others think that if they refrain from doing wrong things, their discipline may offset other areas where they have upset God. Still others think that God deals in spiritual misdemeanors and felonies, and if they are guilty of only the "little" offenses, they will be safe when facing God's judgment.

However, the Bible teaches that for those who expect to be judged according to their effort, their only hope is perfection. Even one error is sufficient to separate them forever from God, who has no imperfection and allows no flaw into his presence. God is aware of every good deed because he is the Creator of goodness. However, no detail of any person's life escapes his attention, and he is fully aware of every violation against him. He knows every thought, attitude, behavior, and action that expresses rebellion against his holiness.

Throughout history, God has intervened to show people that he provides a way for them to escape being judged by their own works. God gave the world numerous prophets who spoke for him, telling the people that they needed God's forgiveness to have heaven. They were told to stop doing the things that were rebellious. Later, God gave the world the Ten Commandments, as well as the additional 603 commands listed in the Old Testament's first five books. It was impossible never to commit an offense. Nonetheless, countless people have tried to live by an impossible standard of perfection. Consequently, they have had to face God's judgment with only their efforts as a defense for their disobedience.

The Bible reveals that no person's performance is adequate to accomplish the goal of pleasing God. Even the most illustrious, benevolent, and selfless person is still stained by human nature, which is inherently flawed. No list of accomplishments is satisfactory to overcome even one offense against God. The person hoping to perform well enough to please God on their own merits simply has no hope at all.

Grace is the opposite of works. Grace is the unmerited favor of God. We experience grace when God gives us something we do not deserve and could in no way ever earn. People experience grace in countless ways every day. Grace abounds on the earth, in the air that circulates,

> You cannot make God accept you because of something you do. God accepts sinners only because they have faith in him.
>
> Romans 4:5 CEV

in the sun that shines, in the rain that falls, and in the seasons that change. Grace is demonstrated in the gifts of your life, your family, your work, your home, and your experiences. God's grace is abundant and amazing. Beyond common grace, God also demonstrates specific grace. This type of grace is perfectly pictured in God's eternal judgment bench, where he examines a person to be fit for heaven.

Myth Buster

Many people think that a person must do good works to demonstrate his worth to God to deserve heaven and God's pleasure. Interestingly, the Bible does teach that it is important for a person to do good works. These works are described as charity, benevolence, or self-sacrifice. However, the Bible also teaches that these works are not a means for earning God's commendation and that they are inadequate to offset or overcome the offenses a person has committed against God. Instead, God gives people opportunities to do good works that express God's grace to other people.

Points to Remember

- Works are considered efforts on a person's part to try to earn God's favor. This could include doing "good things" and refraining from doing "bad things."

- Grace is God's blessing given to a person according to God's initiative. Nothing the person does can earn God's grace.

Check Your Understanding

- **Why are works inadequate to please God?**

Human effort and discipline are insufficient to overcome anyone's offenses against God. These offenses demand judgment apart from human effort.

- **What does it mean that grace is given at God's initiative?**

According to his good and holy nature, God gives grace freely to anyone who will receive it. This gift of grace empowers a person to perform deeds that are good.

- **How is the notion of spiritual misdemeanors and felonies incorrect?**

The Bible teaches that any offense against God deserves punishment. There are no "little" offenses or "big" offenses. There are only offenses, and any offense will be judged. People have two hopes in the physical life—either to be perfect, or to rely upon the grace of God.

- **What's the difference between humanity's ways of thinking about judgment and God's?**

People have always tried to please God through their efforts. But God judges by a different standard. He considers whether a person has accepted his offer of Jesus. Humanity's way is works, but God's plan is grace.

The Trial of Judgment—Standing Before God

Every man, woman, and child who ever lived will eventually have a face-to-face encounter with God. Whether influenced by popular television programs or by actual experiences, some people imagine a stern, black-robed Judge, gavel in hand, ready to pronounce guilt for the least infraction. Even though much of today's legal system is built upon biblical principles, the future trial of judgment will be far more extraordinary than anything real or imagined in the human court of law.

✳

There will be two judgments. The first judgment occurs instantly at the moment of physical death; the second judgment will occur at some point still in the future. At death, every person is placed straightaway in heaven or hell. This immediate judgment is a judgment of the person's faith, not of the person's works.

The LORD is in His holy temple. Let all the earth be silent before Him.

Habakkuk 2:20 NASB

If a person dies without accepting God's forgiveness offered through faith in Jesus, that person is immediately assigned to be apart from God. However, if a person dies having accepted God's grace provision, his soul is immediately assigned to be with God. While these judgments are temporary, they are irrevocable. The good news is that no person immediately placed in heaven will ever later be sent to hell. The

Your former friends are surprised when you no longer plunge into the flood of wild and destructive things they do. . . . But remember that they will have to face God, who will judge everyone, both the living and the dead.

1 Peter 4:4–5 NLT

initial judgment at physical death assigns the eternal destination of each person. Judgment of that person's faith in the physical life foreshadows the second, eternal judgment of God on the person's works.

The purpose and consequence of the second judgment are different for those people in heaven than for those people in hell. The Bible reveals that hell is the temporary home for the condemned. The individual in hell lives there in isolation apart from God until the time of God's final judgment begins. The Bible tells of this great day of judgment when every person in hell will gain a final audience before God. These people are identified as "the dead." At this future time, each of "the dead" will be judged according to his works, or the things he did in the physical life. Every person's deeds—good and bad according to God's reckoning—will be recorded in a collection of books that will be the basis for judgment. When God issues judgment based upon these books, there will be no objection and no overruling. This second judgment is known as the great white throne judgment. God's judgment will be perfect, and his verdict will be final.

Everyone who was initially placed in heaven will also face a future day of judgment by God. These people are known as "the great multitude in heaven." Everyone who is part of this great multitude will dwell in heaven until that time of final judgment. Then these people, too, will face God. However, whereas those among "the dead" will be judged for punishment, "the great multitude in heaven" will be judged for rewards, which will be distributed on an individual basis.

Every act by every individual will be assessed in these judgments. Deeds done by the individual only to impress God will be judged unacceptable. However, any act done as a response to faith will be rewarded. The Bible declares that all Christians will be commended for one faith deed or another, but it makes no promises that Christians will be rewarded equally. This second judgment is known as the rewards judgment. Only the people whose names are found in God's Book of Life will receive heaven and heaven's rewards. Following this judgment, the people so rewarded will be given entrance into the eternal heaven in the presence of God.

People disagree about the timing and sequence of these events. Some people think that the faith judgments and the works judgments happen at the same time following physical death. Other people think these events happen consecutively, but also immediately. Many people hold to the idea that God's faith judgments happen instantly upon physical death, but that the works judgments of God will take place at a date prophesied some time after Jesus' future return to the earth. Even though there is disagreement about when or what comes first, everyone agrees that the faith judgment and works judgment will take place.

> Each of us will give an account of himself to God.
>
> Romans 14:12 HCSB

Digging Deeper

For the person in heaven awaiting final judgment and reward, there is much to look forward to. The Bible declares that a person's faith is credited to them as righteousness. This means that God is pleased by a person whose faith trusts in the promises of God. God rewards that faith in heaven forever in ways that are not fully understood in this life. When faith is the foundation of life, however, all the deeds done as a response to faith are pleasing to God.

Points to Remember

- Every person faces immediate judgment by God based on his faith. This first judgment instantly determines whether he will dwell in heaven or in hell until the final judgment.

- The future day of final judgment is based upon the person's works. For the non-Christian, this is a judgment of condemnation; for the Christian, it is a judgment of reward.

Check Your Understanding

- **What is the Book of Life, and why is it important to judgment?**

The Book of Life records the names of people who have received God's grace through faith in Jesus Christ. Everyone whose name is written in the Book of Life will be permitted into heaven.

- **What is the main difference between the great white throne judgment and the rewards judgment?**

The great white throne judgment is where the condemned will be judged according to their faith and be separated from God forever. The rewards judgment is where Christians will be rewarded for the works they have done while living.

- **How are the immediate faith judgments of God related to the eventual works judgments of God?**

God's initial judgment of a person's faith establishes the person's immediate eternal destination. The subsequent judgment of the person's works establishes the person's final condemnation or reward.

FAQ—What Happens When the Verdict Is "Guilty!"?

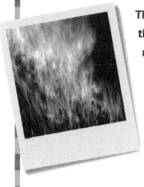

The Bible reveals that many people will one day learn that human efforts to please God are not enough. This means that these people's lives were built upon faulty notions. The gravest of consequences await these people because they will spend eternity in the harshest, most isolated locale imaginable—hell. Hell was not designed for people—it was designed for Satan—but it is altogether secure to imprison anyone who rebels against God. There, the condemned lament, forever apart from God.

All people who go to hell will eventually face judgment for their works. When that happens, God will condemn them to the lake of fire. Originally created as a place of torment for the fallen, rebellious angel Lucifer and his demonic cohorts, the lake of fire is the final place of sorrow. The place now known as hell will itself be cast into the lake of fire. The angels of God will cast the damned into the lake of fire, where they will suffer forever.

The Bible explains this unhappy place in the starkest of terms. It is called "the outer darkness." It is known as a place of "wailing and gnashing of teeth." It is described as a place of eternal thirst, where its inhabitants are perpetually parched, forever unable to cool their dry and burning throats. According to Christ's insightful account of the rich man and Lazarus, hell will have an eternal view of heaven's wonder, yet it will have no means for condemned

> Those who grew up "in the faith" but had no faith will find themselves out in the cold, outsiders to grace and wondering what happened.
>
> Matthew 8:12 MSG

> The one who refuses to believe in the Son will not see life; instead, the wrath of God remains on him.
>
> John 3:36 HCSB

persons to cross the expanse separating the two places. Hell is a place of everlasting torment. To be cast into the lake of fire is to receive God's judgment, which is called the "second death."

Points to Remember

- The people initially judged to go to hell will eventually be cast into the lake of fire, along with Satan and hell itself.

- The "second death" is God's final judgment on people who are cast into the lake of fire after their efforts in the physical life are unable to satisfy God justice.

Check Your Understanding

- **What do the descriptions of hell and the lake of fire reveal about eternity apart from God?**

Unrelenting suffering, sorrow, loneliness, and misery will mark eternity apart from God.

- **Why does it matter that hell was not made for humans?**

The fact that hell was made for rebellious angels shows that God's desire is for all humans to receive the gift of heaven and avoid hell altogether. Hell imprisons people only when they choose to remain in rebellion against God.

FAQ—What Happens When the Verdict Is "Forgiven!"?

For the people who are fortunate enough to have accepted God's forgiveness during their physical lives, the eternal life will be an endless time of blessing and reward. Every Christian will experience the initial faith judgment and be rewarded with immediate entrance into heaven. Each Christian will also experience a future judgment, where every deed done in the physical life will be reviewed and the person will be rewarded. For the Christian, God also promises a future reward of a new, perfect eternal body to replace the imperfect body that died the physical death.

Every person who receives God's forgiveness while living experiences the immediate judgment of faith by being rewarded with heaven. The Bible describes heaven as "Abraham's bosom," "the Father's house," "the heavenly country," "paradise," "the holy place," and "home." These titles indicate that heaven is the place God designed for humans and that God's desire is to live with people forever.

The promise to enter the place of rest is still good, and we must take care that none of you miss out.

Hebrews 4:1 CEV

Surely my just reward is with the LORD, and my work with my God.

Isaiah 49:4 NKJV

At an unknown time in the future, God will gather all of heaven's residents for a time of final judgment. All of these citizens already enjoy God's eternal acceptance. At that time, God will judge each person's deeds done during the physical life. This is in keeping with the nature of God, who judges every detail of every person's life. God will credit good, faithful works as a reward to the person who does such deeds. This judgment will be a time where lost opportunities and foolish mistakes are realized and judged, but it will also be a time of rejoicing and commendation. Even though people will not receive the same reward, every person in heaven will enjoy some measure of praise from God for their faith.

Following the final judgment, all of heaven's people will be rewarded with a new, eternal physical body that will not corrupt the way the current physical body does. This added reward is an expression of God's full restoration of humanity to his original design. Every restored person will live with God forever in a new heaven.

Points to Remember

- Initial entry into heaven is a faith judgment given to all people who believe in the forgiveness God offered through faith in Jesus.

- God will eventually establish a new heaven where he will live forever with all the occupants of the temporary heaven. This will fully restore everything that human rebellion ruined.

Check Your Understanding

- **What is the significance of some of the biblical names for heaven?**

The biblical names for heaven indicate that it is God's home, that it is good, and that it is a place designed for people to dwell with their Creator forever.

- **Why is God's final judgment on the works of heaven's citizens even necessary?**

The future judgment of the faithful is necessary because God's character demands that a person's every deed be evaluated. For the person in heaven, this will bring remorse over missed opportunities and rejoicing over what God rewards.

FAQ—What Are the Common Excuses That God Rejects?

God alone knows the number of people who have gone to the grave since creation. Every one of these people has already faced an initial faith judgment and is in either the temporary hell or heaven. Likewise, everyone who has died will face a future judgment where his life's efforts will be either condemned or rewarded. Commonly, people who are still living have made numerous objections to protest the inevitable judgment of God. Even though the Bible says that every person will be speechless before God's judgment, the Bible records that he has already overruled the most typical objections voiced by the living.

A common argument is that not all people have any or adequate exposure to God's offer of forgiveness. This is a particularly popular argument regarding people who live in non-Christian countries. Surely, this argument goes, God could not or would not assign a person to hell if while still living that person did not hear or know about Jesus. The Bible offers God's rebuttal.

> Since the creation of the world His invisible attributes are clearly seen . . . so that they are without excuse.
>
> Romans 1:20 NKJV
>
> Day and night they never stop, saying: Holy, holy, holy, Lord God, the Almighty, who was, who is, and who is coming.
>
> Revelation 4:8 HCSB

God's eternal goodness demonstrates that he desires that no person die without accepting his gift of forgiveness. God declared that he has revealed enough of himself to all people throughout all time that no person will have an excuse in the time of final judgment. God defines himself by his justice and his mercy. He alone knows the fullness of a person's opportunities versus his response to those opportunities. God will always judge appropriately, and no person who belongs in heaven will ever find himself in hell.

A second common argument is that the very notion of hell runs contrary to the concept of an all-loving God. The thought of hell seems mean, punitive, and perhaps even evil. This view comes from a mistaken understanding of God's nature. It is true that God is an all-loving God. His love surpasses all understanding. Every characteristic of God, including his love, is fully understood in the context of his primary characteristic of holiness. God's love is a holy love. Because of this, if a person's actions or efforts violate God's holiness, the person stands in conviction of that offense. God never compromises his holiness, not even for his love, because his love is based in holiness. God's holiness is what makes heaven perfect; God's holiness underpins all the attributes of God, including his love.

A third, but by no means final, argument is that a person does not have to be perfectly good as long as he is simply better than other people are. It is argued that a person may not be perfect or even good, but at least the person is not as bad as someone else is. On this scale of relativity, a person could compare himself to a thief, a murderer, or some other notorious personality. Interestingly, the Bible recalls that the Roman governor Pontius Pilate gave the people of Jerusalem a relative choice between freeing the guiltless Jesus or the disreputable man Barabbas. The people demonstrated their inherited rebellion against God when they chose to put an innocent Jesus on the cross and to free a guilty Barabbas.

God does not judge a person on a standard of relativity. He does not judge a person based upon how good he is as compared to another person. God does not even compare how good a person could have been if he had made better choices. The self-made person has no hope for pleasing God because God accepts only the person who receives his forgiveness.

The idea that a person can argue with God's judgment is a timeless but flawed belief. The final judgment is different from earthly legal proceedings. In the final judgment, all the evidence has already been recorded. Details of every life will be presented. No person will enter heaven or hell carrying a secret—a secret from God is simply not possible. Every

> "Can anyone hide from me in a secret place? Am I not everywhere in all the heavens and earth?" says the LORD.
>
> Jeremiah 23:24 NLT

hidden thing will be revealed and judged. Every single act, no matter how small or how large, will be commended or condemned. Each single person will be judged on the evidence. No exceptions. No arguments. For those who have been forgiven, the evidence will demonstrate that Jesus' effort alone is sufficient to overturn any evidence that otherwise would have brought forth conviction.

Myth Buster

Many people believe that going to heaven automatically means there will be no more tears and no more sorrow, based upon a promise declared in Revelation 21:4: "He will wipe away every tear from their eyes; and there will no longer be any death; there will no longer be any mourning, or crying, or pain" (NASB). However, this promise is given following God's day of judgment. This may indicate that even people who go to heaven will still have a time of regret and sorrow as part of the rewards judgment as Jesus judges their missed opportunities and foolish disobedience against God. As people recount their life's errors, all these secrets will be revealed. Thankfully, God's forgiveness covers everything.

Points to Remember

• God does not judge people on any scale of relativity. His standard for judgment is absolute and unchanging. He judges people against the standard of his holiness.

- Nobody will be able to use their ignorance of God as an excuse for their rebellion against him. God is merciful and will judge every person appropriately.

- God's love is contained within God's holiness. God loves every person with a perfect love that does not tolerate offenses against his holiness. Because of his holy nature, God is able to love everybody enough to forgive the offenses against him.

Check Your Understanding

- **Why must every offense be judged according to God's holy love?**

If even one offense were to pass without judgment, it would accompany the person into heaven where sin is not allowed. This is simply not possible.

- **How has God revealed himself and his plan to all people?**

While all the ways that God has revealed himself to all people are unknown by all people, every person will stand before God fully understanding how God revealed his plan to him during the physical life. Whatever those circumstances, God has determined them to be sufficient for the person to have responded to God's invitation.

- **Why is relativity an inadequate measure of judgment?**

Relativity suggests that some offenses are more tolerable or more offensive than others. To God, all offenses must be judged equally, since any offense disqualifies a person from heaven. God's grace sufficiently overcomes every offense.

FAQ—Are We Already in Heaven or Hell?

At home and abroad, each day is marked by murder, theft, violence, terrorism, and wars. Some people think that today's world is a literal hell-on-earth and that the afterlife could certainly not be any worse. At the same time, charity and sacrifice can be found. Benevolence and mercy exist. The blessings in the current existence lead some people to perceive this life on earth as heaven, with no belief that the afterlife has anything better to offer. The reality is, however, that the modern world— good and bad—proves that God is real, his judgment is real, and the biblical descriptions of the afterlife are accurate.

The problem of evil upon the earth has plagued humans ever since Adam and Eve first rebelled against God. Because of Satan's deception, people have experienced the horrors of evil. Adam and Eve's son Cain was the first murderer, and their son Abel was the first murder victim. After that, violence spread rampantly through successive generations. Individuals are victimized, groups are persecuted, and entire races have been eradicated. Abductions and slavery— child slavery and white slavery—are horrific but hidden evils. Hatred, jealousy, animosity, racism, prejudice, oppression, and greed are timeless realities.

He makes His sun rise on the evil and on the good, and sends rain on the just and on the unjust.

Matthew 5:45 NKJV

Though they dig into hell, from there My hand shall take them; though they climb up to heaven, from there I will bring them down.

Amos 9:2 NKJV

The result of these never-ending problems is the emergence of an incorrect belief that the physical reality of life on earth is in fact hell and that no afterlife could be worse. First, this mistaken belief leads people to think that rebellious, disobedient actions have no consequences in the afterlife. Second, it is impossible for goodness to be found in hell. All goodness comes from God. The Bible reveals that hell is totally and eternally isolated and separated from God. The fact that goodness exists on the earth—as seen in acts of kindness, mercy, charity, and service— proves that hell on earth is impossible. Third, the notion that people have faith in hell is cynical, rebellious, and wrong. The Bible teaches that faith is absent in hell because eternal separation from God and the hopelessness of hell are understood. The people in hell know that God exists—faith is no longer needed. Fourth, it is simply an incorrect understanding that evil will flourish in hell the way it does on earth. In truth, hell is the place where all the evil that has occurred throughout history is punished. Moreover, hell is home to the evildoers.

The fact that evil exists in the physical realm is evidence that the claims of Christianity are valid. God saw that humans are mired in this evil. Every person perpetrates evil of some sort, whether petty or enormous in human eyes. Jesus' death satisfied God's judgment against evil offenses. His sacrifice freed people to live apart from evil during their physical lives on earth and to return to God in heaven when they die.

Some people mistakenly believe that the current life on earth is in fact heaven. The only evidence for this is the demonstration of goodness that exists upon the earth, as seen by acts of kindness and generosity. There is much good to be found in this life: the love of families, the friendships of neighbors, the joy of music and celebrations, the thrills of accomplishments, the community of God's people. However, demonstration of good on the earth does not prove that earth is heaven; it merely demonstrates that God's grace and mercy are unfolding evidence of his love for humans. All the good in the world cannot offset, discard, or overcome the evil in this world. The Bible describes heaven as a place where there are no more tears, death, sorrow, or rebellion. There is no evil in heaven, so life on earth cannot be life in heaven.

Until God draws time to a close, evil will exist on the earth. God's goodness will still be released upon the earth. Accordingly, good things

> Those eighteen in Jerusalem the other day, the ones crushed and killed when the Tower of Siloam collapsed and fell on them, do you think they were worse citizens than all other Jerusalemites? Not at all. Unless you turn to God, you too will die.
>
> Luke 13:4–5 MSG

will happen to bad people and bad things will happen to good people. In eternity, however, God will reward the faithful and judge the evil. Until then, all people have the opportunity to discover truth, embrace God's invitation, and tell others about his love. In doing this, God's children share the hope that others on the earth may one day experience heaven with God.

Digging Deeper

While heaven exists separately from earth, Christianity offers people a way to experience a small sense of heaven even while living. Heaven is where God lives and humans live with him. When a person becomes a Christian, the Bible says that God's Spirit lives within that person and never leaves. This means that Christians experience the rest of life by faith as close to God as they choose to be and have access to God's love, guidance, and provision throughout their physical lives.

Points to Remember

- Hell is an eternal reality separate from the current earth. Believing that the current earth is hell is a false teaching that denies the reality of the eternal hell and disregards the evidence of God's continuing work on earth.

- Heaven is an eternal reality separate from the current earth. Believing that the current earth is heaven is also a false teaching that denies the promise of eternal heaven. It also disregards the reality of evil and the problem of human rebellion against God on the earth.

- The Bible accurately depicts the current earth as well as the future reality of heaven and earth.

Check Your Understanding

- **Why isn't the current reality hell?**

The current reality cannot be hell because there is good on the earth and people still demonstrate faith. God's presence can be experienced on earth, which is not possible in hell.

- **Why isn't the current reality heaven?**

The current reality cannot be heaven because there is evil on the earth that God has not fully judged. Heaven is a place where God will be fully experienced, which is not the case on the current earth.

- **Why is it important to understand that the current reality is neither heaven nor hell?**

It is important to understand the current reality as a time where faith is grown and developed. A person can experience a relationship with God that will eventually allow that person to go to heaven for eternity and avoid hell altogether, even after having experienced the troubles of evil in the physical life.

FAQ—What About Those Who Never Heard About Jesus?

With the world population approaching seven billion people, millions of people have never been told that Jesus came to forgive their rebellion against God and offer them the gift of heaven. People in nearly every culture are not aware that the Bible even exists. Yet, God says that he will judge each person of the world solely on whether they believe that Jesus is Lord. The Bible explains more fully what that means and exactly why God's standard is so stringent.

✳

A typical objection among people in parts of the world where Christianity is established and accepted is an apparent deep concern for people where the gospel of Jesus is unknown and infrequently shared. They want to know how God can judge people by whether or not they believe that Jesus is God in the flesh if in fact they have never even heard about Jesus. Human logic and human reasoning suggest that it is unfair for God to do so. If God were to behave so unfairly, it is reasoned, then it would not make sense to worship him. The operative word here is *human—human* logic, *human* reasoning.

This common question springs from a misunderstanding about human nature. It assumes a good and altruistic human morality. It reasons that all people are good and deserve equal opportunities to discover God. Most important, it suggests that the person asking the question is particularly good. Why? Simply because he is asking the question, perhaps

No one can have faith without hearing the message about Christ. . . . The Scriptures say, "The message was told everywhere on earth. It was announced all over the world."

Romans 10:17–18 CEV

You will be my witnesses, telling people about me everywhere . . . to the ends of the earth.

Acts 1:8 NLT

even as an advocate of the unknown other who may not have the same opportunity to learn biblical truth, the person establishes himself as the standard. However, no one is born "good." The Bible says that because of flawed human nature, every person is born with a soul that is oriented toward disobedience, rebellion, and hell. Every person falls short of God's standard. Consider Romans 3:23: "All of us have sinned and fallen short of God's glory" (CEV). Nobody gets to heaven on his own. Every person strays from goodness. The penalty for all rebellion and any disobedience is death and eternal separation from God.

In addition, the question presumes that every person must learn about God's truth in the same way. The Bible says that God has revealed himself to all people from the beginning of time and that no person will have an excuse for disbelieving. According to the Bible, God revealed himself in the creation of the universe as well as in the creation of human life (that people are made in the image of God). Many people find the basis for their faith in the majesty of the mountains, the exquisite colors of the sunset, the grandeur of the prairies. God has consistently used supernatural means to share his plans with people, including such resources as dreams, angelic messengers, prophets, and supernatural phenomena. The Bible records that at different times God has used a giant fish (the story of Jonah), a donkey temporarily given the gift of speech (the story of Balaam, the donkey, and the angel), and even a vine-chewing worm (back to Jonah again!) to convey what he wanted people to know about himself.

The truth is that God loves everyone. He wants all people to turn away from their natural tendencies to rebel. He wants people to come to him by faith. God desires a real relationship with every person and offers heaven to everyone who will accept it on his terms.

Around the world at this moment, Christians are faithfully telling the story of Jesus and his love and sacrifice. The Bible describes God as patient and promises that he will come again to close out human history when all nations have heard about Jesus. Not every person will hear Christ's story in exactly the same way or the same number of times.

Pray for us . . . that the Lord's message may spread rapidly and be honored, just as it was with you.

2 Thessalonians 3:1 HCSB

But by whatever methods God chooses, when every person stands before God at the end of the physical life, God will rightly and fairly judge him.

Digging Deeper

God's primary plan for communicating his gospel to the world is to use people to share it with others. This has been his main method for rescuing souls since the time of Jesus, whose final command to his followers was to spread the message of his love and salvation to the entire world. God's strategy for telling those people who live in isolated places of the world relies upon the obedience of Christians to talk about the difference God has made in their lives.

Points to Remember

- God's global strategy for rescuing people from hell and giving them heaven uses means that he has made available to himself expressly for this purpose.

- God does not promise that every person will learn about his plan the same way. He has made provision for everyone to have adequate opportunities to learn the truth and respond to God.

- God has used unusual and even supernatural methods to reveal himself and his truth to people throughout history.

Check Your Understanding

- **How will God judge all people based on whether or not they believe that Jesus is God?**

The Bible declares that the entire world will have been told the truth about Jesus and that God will rightly judge the world according to what he has revealed.

- **How is God's plan communicated throughout the world and down through history?**

The message of Jesus Christ has been primarily communicated from person to person using human relationships throughout history. Typically, a person will come to a faith belief that Jesus is God because of what someone else has said about his own personal experience in this matter.

- **What does it mean that God has at times used supernatural means to communicate his message?**

The Bible records that God has been actively involved in revealing himself, his plan, and his truth to people throughout history. He has periodically done so in dramatic, miraculous, and unexplainable ways.

FAQ—Is Purgatory Real?

All Christians agree that real holiness—cleansing or purifying—is required before entering the presence of God. For most Protestants, holiness is a one-time happening; for Catholics and others, holiness is a process. Purgatory refers to this process.

The doctrine of purgatory teaches that few people are spiritually prepared for heaven—holy—at the point of death. According to this traditional belief, most people must go through a time of spiritual purification called purgatory.

Purgatory is a difficult and controversial concept within Christianity. The difficulty comes from the idea that purgatory is a *place* rather than a *process*. It is popularly thought that purgatory is a specific location between heaven and hell where a person goes after death to be spiritually purified. Most Protestants do not believe there is any such place. Surprising to some, however, Catholics do not specify that purgatory is a place.

The notion of an actual place is based upon centuries-old tradition.

> Christ is the only foundation. Whatever we build on that foundation will be tested by fire on the day of judgment. Then everyone will find out if we have used gold, silver, and precious stones, or wood, hay, and straw. We will be rewarded if our building is left standing. But if it is destroyed by the fire, we will lose everything. Yet we ourselves will be saved, like someone escaping from flames.
>
> 1 Corinthians 3:11–15 CEV

> The poor man died and was carried by the angels to be with Abraham. The rich man also died and was buried, and his soul went to the place of the dead.
>
> Luke 16:22–23 NLT

In the Middle Ages, even before the Protestant Reformation, the church tried to spell out its doctrine of purgatory, deliberately keeping away from any words that might be misunderstood to refer to purgatory as a place. In 1968, it tried again to clarify its teaching of purgatory as a purging "process."

The idea of purgatory is rooted in ancient Jewish traditions where people prayed for the dead. It was believed that all people went to a common grave called sheol, which is akin to but not the same as purgatory. Some Jewish rabbis taught that it was possible to pray for the dead that their offenses against God would be forgiven. This practice is recorded in the apocryphal book 2 Maccabees 12:39-45, but there is no specific mention of purgatory in the canonical Old Testament or the New Testament books.

The word *purgatory* is from the Latin *purgatorio,* which means "cleansing" or "purifying." Several verses in the Bible refer to cleansing and purification.

Digging Deeper

Many of the concepts of purgatory have been shaped by the imagination of artists and authors rather than by biblical texts. Perhaps the most famous of all influencers was the fourteenth-century Florentine poet Dante Alighieri, who is best known for his epic trilogy about the afterlife. *Inferno* is a frightening, yet fanciful picture of hell, complete with multiple levels sorting rebellious souls according to their offenses. *Paradiso* portrays his own vision of heaven. These two works bookend *Purgatorio,* his epic novel of purgatory represented as a mountain where Christians climb terraces toward purification and enlightenment.

A common misconception is the idea that heaven and hell are divided into different regions. The imagery painted is of a multileveled heaven where common people experience the lowest levels of bliss, while the "penthouse" of heaven is reserved for God, the angels, and the holiest of human saints. Conversely, a tiered hell sorts out damnation and punishment according to a mystic scale of evil, with the worst offenses being punished more harshly than lesser offenses. As fanciful as this may be, there is simply no biblical basis for degrees of heaven and grades of hell.

Religious traditions and cultural influences have created and shaped the perception of multilevel afterlife destinations. Entire religions have based their beliefs about the afterlife on these cultural influences. Buddhism, Hinduism, Mormonism, and Jehovah's Witnesses are just some of the religions that teach that the afterlife offers different planes of heaven, hell, or both.

Even within Christianity, erroneous beliefs shape everyday behavior, sometimes for generations. Many scholars believe that author Dante Alighieri's fourteenth-century *Divine Comedy* represented common thinking during medieval times regarding heaven and hell. He presented hell as a domain of nine descending concentric circles, each level reserved for increasingly despicable offenses. The centermost level at the center of the earth contained the betrayers, where Satan—imprisoned in a lake of ice—forever tortures

I heard a voice thunder from the Throne: "Look! Look! God has moved into the neighborhood, making his home with men and women!"

Revelation 21:3 MSG

At the time of harvest I will say to the reapers, "First gather together the tares and bind them in bundles to burn them, but gather the wheat into my barn."

Matthew 13:30 NKJV

Judas for betraying Jesus. Heaven is likewise imagined as nine spheres, each level embracing a higher virtue, with God existing above the highest sphere.

Interestingly, the Bible does speak of "three heavens," which has led some people and even different religions to conclude that God has three different heavens or three levels of the same heaven. However, the context of these biblical passages reveals that these terms are simply being used to describe different aspects of the wholeness of God's creation. The "first heaven" mentioned in the Bible is understood to be the sky and atmosphere of the earth. This consists of the air that humans and animals breathe, the sky that holds the clouds, and the sky that extends approximately seven miles above the surface of the earth.

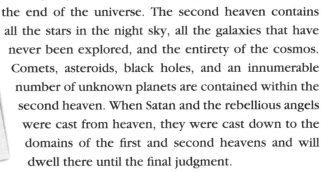

The "second heaven" is a coined term to explain the realm of space that begins immediately beyond the earthly atmosphere and extends to the end of the universe. The second heaven contains all the stars in the night sky, all the galaxies that have never been explored, and the entirety of the cosmos. Comets, asteroids, black holes, and an innumerable number of unknown planets are contained within the second heaven. When Satan and the rebellious angels were cast from heaven, they were cast down to the domains of the first and second heavens and will dwell there until the final judgment.

The "third heaven" is God's dwelling place. It is the true heaven as most commonly understood in theological terms. It begins immediately at the end of the second heaven, and nobody on this side of eternity knows the breadth and depth of its dimensions. The only things that are known, understood, or believed about the third heaven have been revealed by the timeless testimonies recorded in the Bible. While the terminology expressed in the Bible speaks of three heavens, the first two speak of the known realms of sky and space, and only the third is actually heaven.

No such distinctions are offered in the biblical presentation of hell that awaits those who are destined to be there for eternity. It is described in singularly miserable terms with a message of absolute sorrow for every person who is there. There is no relief from this in a "lesser hell," and there is no greater punishment in a "worse hell." To be in hell is to be separated from God, forever imprisoned in a lake of fire.

The Bible reveals hell and heaven each as a single domain. Logically and theologically, it is unreasonable for God to grade realms of either location. To do so would come at the expense of the Bible's revealed message of God's absolute opposition to all rebellion and evil. It would also come at the expense of the Bible's message of God's perfect love for all people based solely on his holy nature and not on human performance. To enter heaven is the greatest reward available to every person. All who go to heaven will forever be fully in the presence of God. Everyone there will experience the fullness of joy.

> I was caught up to the third heaven fourteen years ago. . . . I do know that I was caught up to paradise.
>
> 2 Corinthians 12:2–4 NLT

Points to Remember

- Concepts of heaven and hell as having multiple levels of punishment or reward are based in conjecture. These nonbiblical ideas have resulted in relativistic thinking influencing everyday behavior.

- Heaven and hell are single-level domains where punishment is separation from God, and reward is eternal life with God.

- Where the Bible mentions "different" heavens, it is actually referring to the sky and to space as realms below heaven.

Something to Ponder

 A modern popular phenomenon is the publicized first-hand accounts of people who claim to have temporarily died and ascended to heaven. While the validity of these claims is subject to opinion, they are merely the latest to copy what the apostles Paul and John themselves claimed to have experienced. Both men are recorded in the Bible as having experiences of being taken to heaven. Furthermore, several Old Testament prophets experienced heavenly visions. While many modern accounts seem to contradict the message of the Bible, every biblical testimony agrees that heaven is a place where God's love and God's holiness are exemplified.

Check Your Understanding

- **What does Christianity teach regarding the levels of heaven and hell?**

Christianity teaches that heaven and hell are single-level domains where a person is either with God or separated from God forever.

- **Why is the biblical teaching that heaven and hell are single-level domains important?**

The biblical teaching that heaven and hell are single-level domains is important so that people do not mistakenly think that they are "good" or "bad" relative to other people; rather, people should base their understanding solely upon their relationship with God.

- **What does it mean that heaven is the "third heaven"?**

While the first and second "heavens" are skies and space, respectively, the "third heaven" is where heaven actually begins. Its description means that it is higher and farther beyond any known, measurable, or humanly discoverable location.

FAQ—Does Everyone Get to Go to Heaven?

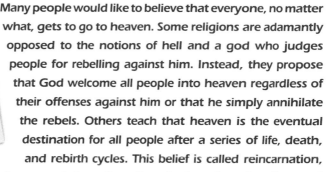

Many people would like to believe that everyone, no matter what, gets to go to heaven. Some religions are adamantly opposed to the notions of hell and a god who judges people for rebelling against him. Instead, they propose that God welcome all people into heaven regardless of their offenses against him or that he simply annihilate the rebels. Others teach that heaven is the eventual destination for all people after a series of life, death, and rebirth cycles. This belief is called reincarnation, where people learn from the mistakes of previous lives and eventually attain the perfection necessary to enter heaven.

The Bible teaches that heaven is populated by people who, while living the physical life, trusted the sufficiency of God's forgiveness. Jesus taught that God gave all people the opportunity to avoid hell. He taught that every person would experience a resurrection from the dead and that every person would either be granted entrance into heaven or be separated from God and delivered to hell. He described the way to heaven in exclusive terms and warned that people who took the more common path would be eternally separated from God.

The gate is small and the way is narrow that leads to life, and there are few who find it.

Matthew 7:14 NASB

Is anyone thirsty? Come! All who will, come and drink, drink freely of the Water of Life!

Revelation 22:17 MSG

The Bible reveals that heaven will welcome innumerable people who trusted in God's promises by faith throughout the ages. Heaven's citizenry will consist of people from every generation, every nation, and every population. The Bible teaches that some families will be divided because some family members believed in God's promises while others did not. Some lifelong members of Christian churches will find themselves eternally excluded from heaven because they never experienced a faith relationship with God. No person gets to heaven based upon his best efforts, family genealogy, or church membership. Heaven will be the home of every person who accepts God's terms and worships Jesus as Lord.

Points to Remember

- Heaven is available to all people, but many people will choose to be excluded from it by never accepting the offer to be forgiven by God for their disobedience to him.

  - Heaven's population will be vast, consisting of countless individuals who were given entry by God, who gracefully allowed them in because of his love.

Check Your Understanding

- **Why doesn't everybody go to heaven?**

Not everybody goes to heaven because God requires people to follow his plan of forgiveness in order to get there. Without God's forgiveness, heaven is unattainable.

- **If not everybody goes to heaven, what is important to know about who does go to heaven?**

It is important to know that heaven is available to all people, and every person is given the physical life to receive God's forgiveness. Each person can make the choice to receive God's gift while he or she has the opportunity.

Heaven—Everybody's Hope and God's Promise to Welcome You Home

Heaven is the home of God and the destination of everyone who has accepted his invitation to join him there. Even so, biblical glimpses of the eternal residence defy explanation and comprehension.

Contents

God's Story of Eternity—Heaven Now and
Heaven to Come..81

Perfection Realized—The Environment of Heaven...................85

Watchless and Clockless—The Endlessness of Heaven 89

The Activities in Heaven—The Comings and Goings
in Eternity 91

The Civilization of Heaven—Government and
Community in Eternity 95

FAQ—Does Heaven *Really* Exist? 97

FAQ—Where Is Heaven Located? 99

FAQ—What Does It Means to Praise God for Eternity? 101

FAQ—Is Saint Peter the Doorman of the Pearly Gates? 103

FAQ—Do All Babies Get to Go to Heaven? 105

FAQ—What Will We Eat and Drink in Heaven? 109

The heavens proclaim the glory of God.
The skies display his craftsmanship.

Psalm 19:1 NLT

God's Story of Eternity—Heaven Now and Heaven to Come

It is nearly impossible to think about God without thinking of heaven. After all, heaven is God's home. However, the history of heaven is an important but little-told story that is closely linked with the history of the earth. While heaven and earth are currently separated by the great gap between life and death, they were once intimately connected and will be again in the future. Discovering the history of heaven will strengthen your faith and increase your expectation for being a part of heaven's wonderful future.

The Bible's first words declare that "in the beginning, God created the heavens and the earth." God existed before heaven, and he chose to create heaven as the place for him to live. When God spoke the heavens into existence, he created the earth at the same time, and the two realms were linked. Just as heaven was created to be God's chosen address, the earth was created to be the perfectly appointed garden home for humans, the masterpiece of his creation. After creating Adam and Eve, God interacted with them from heaven, and they enjoyed the blessings of an unimpaired relationship with their Creator.

As it is written: "Eye has not seen, nor ear heard, nor have entered into the heart of man the things which God has prepared for those who love Him."

1 Corinthians 2:9 NKJV

I will declare that your love stands firm forever, that you established your faithfulness in heaven itself.

Psalm 89:2 NIV

This ideal relationship between humans and God in a united heaven and earth was short-lived. Adam and Eve disobeyed God and ate the fruit from the Tree of Knowledge of Good and Evil. This offense forced God to separate heaven from the earth, the perfect from the corrupt.

From that point until now, the only way any person can move from the earth to experience heaven is through death and spiritual rebirth.

From that day to this, heaven remains perfect. It remains God's home. It is described in the Bible as the storehouse of his blessings, of wind and rain, thunder and lightning, and of snow and hail. Heaven is the mantle that holds but does not contain the glory and majesty of God. It is where his throne is established. From his throne, God directs the affairs of human history on earth according to his perfect will.

From his home in heaven, God watches every detail of every moment of every person's life. From his vantage, he sees every potential of life's peaks, valleys, roadblocks, detours, and destinations. From heaven, God hears every word, every prayer spoken and unspoken, every thought entertained, and every motive deliberated. From his encompassing perspective in heaven, God observes everything, understands everything, and controls everything.

As vast and incredible as heaven is, its confines are unable to contain or constrain the fullness of God. The Bible reveals that Jesus left heaven and came to the earth so that people could again experience an unimpaired relationship with God. Jesus taught that heaven is available in the here and now for all who would believe in the promises of God. Jesus promised that God's Holy Spirit could live within every person who humbles himself and submits to God's forgiving authority. These people, though still living physically on earth, would by faith enjoy a spiritual relationship with God and be reunited with him after death.

While Christians can rejoice that God graciously forgives and welcomes people into heaven, the larger and more amazing truth is that God's plan for heaven and earth is not finished. The Bible speaks of a day when the present earth will be destroyed by fire. Following a final judgment upon all of creation, God will create a new heaven and a new earth that will be again and forevermore united.

> Now all we can see of God is like a cloudy picture in a mirror. Later we will see him face to face. We don't know everything, but then we will, just as God completely understands us.
>
> 1 Corinthians 13:12 CEV

A new city of Jerusalem will come down from heaven to the earth. In the center of this city, God's throne will be established, and Jesus will be seated upon it as Lord. The new heaven will be a realm of perpetual light brightened by the radiance of God's glory. This immense expanse will be the full restoration of God's plan. Inhabitants will enjoy unrestrained access to all locations in God's realm and experience a fullness of life scarcely imaginable by the shadows of the life we experience now.

Digging Deeper

The Bible offers spectacular dimensions of the New Jerusalem. In Revelation 21:16, an angel measures the city with a rod and declares the city to be 12,000 cubic stadia. According to ancient measures, one stadium was approximately 600 feet. This means that the New Jerusalem will cover approximately 1,500 miles in every direction, or more than 2.25 million square miles. It will ascend 1,500 miles into the air. The new heaven offers ample room for all history's believers!

Points to Remember

- Heaven was created for people to spend eternity with God.

- Even though heaven and earth are currently separated by life and death, they will one day be reunited according to God's plan.

• Heaven is still available today to anyone who believes in God's ability to finish what he started and responds to God's offer of forgiveness through faith in Jesus.

Check Your Understanding

■ **When were heaven and earth disconnected and why does it matter?**

Heaven and earth were created in unity on the second day of creation, but were separated after the sin of Adam and Eve. Now earth is the dwelling place of man, and heaven is the home of God. This illustrates the seriousness of sin and emphasizes the need for us to be restored back to God.

■ **Why does God have to have heaven?**

God does not have to have heaven. He chose to make heaven and live there. He did so knowing in advance the full work he would have to accomplish to have an eternal relationship with people. This demonstrates the depth of God's vast love for his creation. He went to extraordinary lengths to bless his creation after it broke their perfect relationship with him.

■ **Why does there have to be a new heaven to replace the contemporary heaven that exists now?**

Ultimately, God's plan is to complete the work of redemption. He will redeem that which was broken by Adam and Eve. He will create a new heaven, a new earth, and a New Jerusalem. The events of his judgment and creation are in accordance with his nature and will be complete only following his final judgment upon all of creation.

Perfection Realized—The Environment of Heaven

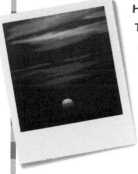

Heaven is a real destination for a multitude of people. The residents of heaven come from every nation, every race, and every social rank, male and female. Heaven is a place of unimaginable beauty, unparalleled peace, and unequaled perfection. It is God's home, where everyone lives in harmony. While heaven may be familiar to the best offerings of the physical world in some respects, it completely transcends and surpasses the present earth in every way.

As the holy home of God, heaven is perfectly suited to his nature. While God is not limited by the boundaries of heaven, heaven is filled completely by the presence of God. Heaven is a place of perfect peace where there is no evil. There is no rebellion, no sin, no death, and no pain. There is no jealousy, no competition, no cheating, no corruption, and no scandal. Heaven's residents are unique and distinct, and all residents like as well as love one another with a pure, holy love.

Heaven is a real place and not just a "state of mind." Heaven is a physical place existing beyond the universe's boundaries, and it is called both "the eternal city" and "the heavenly country." It is home to the Tree of Life, the river of life that flows from the throne of God, and to all of God's creatures, including humans, angels, and animals. Heaven is the home to every person in world history who has been restored by God, from Adam onward to Christians who are passing today from this life to the next.

You have come . . . to the general assembly and church of the first born who are registered in heaven, to God the Judge of all.

Hebrews 12:22–23 NKJV

Blessed are those who dwell in your house; they are ever praising you.

Psalm 84:4 NIV

Heaven is also a place of increased awareness. Some world religions and philosophical beliefs picture heaven as a place of blissful ignorance or restricted understanding, but the Bible indicates that the opposite is true. Every person who goes to heaven will one day have to give an account of every detail of life. This will require memory. In heaven, the human mind is free from the limits of bodily inhibitors, inhibitors like temptations, addictions, and biases. While humans will by no means know in the manner that God knows all, people can expect to know more and to understand what they know even better than ever.

Heaven is a place of continual worship, which is the act of declaring the worth of God. The Bible indicates that God is continuously praised in heaven for his attributes. People and angels will speak and sing their worship to God, honoring his holiness, his love, his might, his justice, and even his wrath. This worship will be an exciting, natural outgrowth of being in the full presence of God. Because there is no rebellion or selfishness, there will be no disagreement over the worship. All worship will be true and directed solely to God. Everything a person does in heaven will be an expression of worship.

One interesting component of worship in heaven is the continuation of the practice of prayer. Prayer is simply communication with God, and this practice will continue in heaven, although in radically different ways since prayer in heaven means speaking to God face-to-face. The Bible speaks of people in heaven praying to God asking for his judgment to come upon the earth. What is prayed for by faith on earth is prayed for in fullness in heaven.

Heaven is a place of celebration. The Bible says that the angels rejoice whenever a person is saved from hell and reoriented to heaven. The Bible speaks of heavenly feasts and marriage celebrations. It is likely that the feasts, festivals, and commemorative celebrations established by God in the Old Testament will forever occur in heaven. All of these festive gatherings will be marked by sharing meals and drink. Wine is served in heaven, but no drunkenness or shameful actions result from drinking it. Every celebration will be a joyful time of community and praise to God.

> There's more joy in heaven over one sinner's rescued life than over ninety-nine good people in no need of rescue.
>
> Luke 15:7 MSG

Heaven is a bustling place of constant activity where people will be given authority and responsibility. We will interact with other people from all generations as well as with angels. In heaven, people will never fatigue, never experience stress, never worry, and will always be productive. Heaven is perfect in every way, even beyond what the imagination can begin to comprehend!

Myth Buster

In all the environment of heaven, some of people's most commonly expected aspects are notoriously absent in the Bible. The Scriptures do not refer to heaven's occupants dressed solely in long, flowing white robes, having wings sprouted from their backs, riding eternally upon clouds, and endlessly strumming harps. These traditions have evolved over centuries as people have confused and merged details about angels with humans and have added nonbiblical hypotheses about the afterlife. What the Bible promises is that people there will have full, perfect God-centered lives that will never end and never be boring.

Points to Remember

- Heaven is completely unlike the earth because there is absolutely no rebellion or disobedience in heaven and it is holy. God's holy presence fills heaven, and the people of heaven live full, active lives.

  - Heaven is a place of perfection in every measure. It far exceeds the human capacity to comprehend the grandeur of its environment.

Check Your Understanding

- **Why is it important to know that heaven is holy?**

It is important to understand that heaven is holy because heaven's perfect holiness is its primary distinguishing characteristic. No other place is holy the way heaven is holy.

- **Why is it necessary for people to worship forever in heaven?**

The perpetual worship that occurs in heaven is not a matter of necessity so much as it is a matter of natural response to the holy goodness of God expressed throughout heaven. All of heaven's inhabitants are perfectly content in heaven, and their natural response to this blessing is to praise God in all things.

- **Why does it matter that people will have responsibility in heaven?**

The responsibility of humans in heaven is important because it shows that God's plan for people extends for all time. It shows that heaven will never be boring and that humans will have a full life forever.

- **What is in heaven?**

Heaven is home to the Tree of Life, the river of life that flows from the throne of God, and to all of God's creatures, including humans, angels, and animals. Heaven is the home to every person in world history who has been restored by God, from Adam onward to Christians who are passing today from this life to the next.

Watchless and Clockless—
The Endlessness of Heaven

The first heaven and second heaven exist within the universe. This means that the dimension of time binds each one. This is why travel from one city to another or one country to another is measured by time. Likewise, even greater expanses of time measure space travel because of the far more distant locations. The third heaven, though, exists outside and beyond the constraints of time. The time dimensions of heaven are mysterious and intriguing, and they offer exciting possibilities to those who will one day call heaven their home.

Heaven has always kept an unconventional timepiece in how it relates to the universal concept of time. Human understanding tells people to pray in the present moment, asking God for an answer to a future event. However, the Bible reveals that God has prepared an answer for the prayer before it has been voiced. Jesus entered into time and died for the offenses of all people, yet the Bible declares him "the Lamb slain from the foundation of the world" (Revelation 13:8 NKJV).

You've got all the time in the world—whether a thousand years or a day, it's all the same to you.

Psalm 90:4 MSG

The world and its desires pass away, but the man who does the will of God lives forever.

1 John 2:17 NIV

The Bible indicates that there will still be measures of time in heaven. Distances will still need to be traveled. Deeds will still be performed, responsibilities will still be fulfilled, and work will still be done. Songs requiring tempo, a measure of time, will be sung. However, heaven is a place where "one day is as a thousand years, and a thousand years as one day" (2 Peter 3:8 NKJV). Efforts to comprehend the measure of heaven's endless time will always fall short from this side of eternity.

In a realm where time will be completely unlike how it is measured and understood in the physical reality, the possibilities are staggering. With the promise that this new, heavenly understanding of time will never end, the citizens of heaven will have forever to explore the limitless opportunities that this new sense of time offers.

Points to Remember

- God is not limited by time in any way, now or in the future eternity. He uses time to accomplish his purposes.

- Time in eternity is far different from time within planetary and universal space on the earth.

- However time will be measured in eternity, the most important constant is that time will never end in heaven.

Check Your Understanding

- **How is time different here on earth than it is in heaven?**

Time on earth is measured in seconds, minutes, hours, days, weeks, months, years, decades, centuries, and so on. These markers are utterly irrelevant and meaningless in heaven, where time is apparently measured in completely different ways, if at all.

- **Why does it matter that time is never-ending, since it is so different?**

The endlessness of heaven is important to understand because, for the inhabitants of heaven, this new measure of time will be without end, offering an everlasting reality full of unimaginable opportunities of discovery.

The Activities in Heaven—The Comings and Goings in Eternity

Eternal heaven promises experiences that far surpass anything faced in the present reality. With humans living in an entirely new creation that includes a new heaven and a new earth, discoveries and exploration will be unprecedented. The heavenly future means living in a reality unlimited by human constraints. With an entirely new understanding of angelic and human interaction—including relating to people of all human history—relationships will be unlike the bonds expressed in our earthly reality. The future of heaven offers incomprehensibly endless horizons.

The eternal heaven is a place where God fulfills his promises of redemption and renewal. Here, God will correct everything that was corrupted through human rebellion against him. On a cosmic scale, the Bible speaks to a future when God establishes eternity and destroys the current earth, which will be replaced by a new earth, free from the curse of human disobedience. The new earth will be paradise, luxurious in every way, and ideal for meeting the needs of all its inhabitants forever.

Furthermore, the current heaven will pass away and give way to the arrival of the eternal heaven. This eternal heaven will encompass the new earth, and the two will not be divided the way the current heaven and earth are separated. In the eternal heaven, there will be no sun and no moon, for all of creation will be illuminated by the unsurpassable radiance of God's glory. The brightness of his holiness is what will fuel the light of heavenly creation. There

In the future, everyone will worship and learn about you, our Lord.

Psalm 22:30 CEV

At the name of Jesus every knee will bow . . . every tongue will confess that Jesus Christ is Lord.

Philippians 2:10–11 NASB

will be no nighttime because there is no time where God will not be fully radiant and present in his unified creation.

Unlike now, humans will be able to travel freely between heaven and earth. The interactive environment in the eternal realm is most fully understood in the promise that God will create an eternal capital city, the New Jerusalem. While division, conflict, and strife mark the current Jerusalem, the New Jerusalem will descend from the new heaven and rest upon the new earth. It will be God's home and, accordingly, will be the primary residence of the citizens of heaven. The finery of the New Jerusalem will be more opulent than the mind can conceive, but its most striking feature will be that from its center, Jesus will reign upon his throne.

Interestingly, the Bible speaks of a future where the kings of the new earth will freely enter the never-closing city gates of the New Jerusalem. This indicates that the eternal future will be characterized by not only unmitigated peace but also continual activity. Humans will be given authority, will bear responsibilities, and will be able to fulfill these expectations without struggle or opposition. The fact that humans will be coming in and going out of the New Jerusalem also demonstrates that humans will be highly active and interactive in the eternal reality. Humans will have authority over angels and will exist in harmony within God's heavenly creation, thus enjoying the redemption that God will successfully accomplish for eternity.

Finally, to fully enjoy the eternal experience, all people who will live in heaven will be given new bodies that are similar to current physical bodies but without the deficiencies that plague the current human condition. The new bodies will consist of flesh, blood, and bone, but heaven's residents will not be corrupted by a nature that opposes God. Accordingly, people will not age, tire, or become sick. They are new, whole, eternal creations in heaven that have complete unity with God.

The biblical image revealed about the postresurrection bodies indicates that the new heavenly bodies may be free from the time and space limitations that restrict people in this present reality. The book of Acts recounts how after his resurrection, Jesus visited his followers, who were gathered in a locked upper room in Jerusalem. Jesus established that he was not a ghost or an apparition by permitting the apostle Thomas to touch the wounds he received from the crucifixion. Jesus also demonstrated the postresurrection ability to travel distances that were impossible by human modes available at the time.

> I also saw the Holy City, new Jerusalem, coming down out of heaven from God, prepared like a bride adorned for her husband.
>
> Revelation 21:2 HCSB

These manifestations of supernatural abilities may be limited to Jesus, or they could be normal physical realities common to all citizens living in the eternal heaven.

Digging Deeper

The common understanding of eternity scarcely does justice to the biblical imagery of its promised greatness. Typical understanding of heaven is limited in its scope and appeal. Yet the Bible reveals that God's intention in redeeming creation is to restore all of creation. This includes God's overhauling the heavenly realm currently given to Satan until the time of final judgment. The eternal heaven will offer an entirely new universe that awaits discovery, fully illuminated by God and offered to humanity for enjoyment.

Points to Remember

- The eternal heaven will consist of the new heaven, the new earth, and the New Jerusalem.

- These realms will be totally integrated and completely interactive environments.

- Our ability to navigate the eternal kingdom likely exceeds our ability to grasp it fully according to current physical limitations.

Check Your Understanding

- **How is the creation of the new earth different from the creation of the new heaven?**

The old heaven will give way to the new heaven, but not in the sense that the old heaven will be destroyed in judgment the way the old earth will be destroyed prior to the creation of the new earth.

- **What is the significance that the New Jerusalem will descend from the new heaven upon the new earth?**

The descent of the New Jerusalem from the new heaven indicates the capital city's holiness. Its descent upon the new earth indicates that the entire heavenly realm is fully interactive for all its citizens.

- **What does it mean that the earth's kings will enter the gates of New Jerusalem?**

Eternity is marked by human responsibility and authority. People will be fully alive and interacting with one another in purposeful, productive ways that glorify God forever.

The Civilization of Heaven—Government and Community in Eternity

Heaven is not simply a locale. It is a place of organized administration and government. The Bible declares that God himself instituted government and that this institution does not pass away with the conclusion of the present earth. In fact, the Bible indicates that before Jesus was ever born, God promised he would one day institute an everlasting government over all creation. God has determined that people serving under Jesus' authority will serve in important positions of leadership and responsibility.

✳

The Jewish people were familiar with the biblical promises of the coming reign of the Messiah. This is one reason why Judaism rejects Jesus as Messiah, because Jesus did not come and institute God's kingdom on earth as promised in prophecy. However, New Testament teachings indicate that this mission objective is an expected aspect upon his return and eternal reign. Jesus is understood to be the ruling monarch in this, and the government will rest securely upon the mantle of his leadership, never to be removed.

> His government and its peace will never end. He will rule with fairness and justice from the throne of his ancestor David for all eternity.
>
> Isaiah 9:7 NLT

> The kingdoms of this world have become the kingdoms of our Lord and of His Christ, and He shall reign forever and ever!
>
> Revelation 11:15 NKJV

In the future heaven, Jesus will rule all creation from his throne in New Jerusalem. However, the new earth will be populated by residents of heaven and ruled by righteous leaders who have been appointed by Jesus himself. Humans will have authority, and government will exist.

The future government will be perfect because it will exist in the heavenly environment where there is no sin, no death, no evil, and no corruption.

The administration of the future heaven will be revolutionary because its leaders will likely be those people who inconspicuously and anonymously committed their physical lives to selflessly serving others without reward or recognition. It will be an administration characterized by total unity between the leaders and the land's citizens because all are residents in heaven under the perfect authority of Jesus.

Points to Remember

- Heaven is ruled by Jesus from his throne in New Jerusalem. He will flawlessly administer his government that will be forever expanding and will never be opposed.

- In the future, humans will have administrative responsibility over God's kingdom under Jesus' authority. They will lead in this perfect environment of peace and cooperation with one another.

Check Your Understanding

- **What is the significance of the future human leadership of God's government?**

It is significant that God chooses his leaders based upon the criteria of humility and service to others and not ambition and self-seeking. God's authorities are those who demonstrated godly character in the physical life.

- **What does it mean that "God instituted government"?**

God is the author of the concept of government and the implementer of it in the affairs of humans. This parallels the belief that God is orderly and not chaotic. He offers government as a way for people to be orderly as he is orderly.

FAQ—Does Heaven *Really* Exist?

It is difficult to imagine a place where there is no rebellion, no sorrow, no death, and no pain. Heaven not only seems to be far away, but it also seems to be an incomprehensible possibility. Perhaps it is difficult to imagine that God exists, much less that he has a home he desires to share with humans. Even for those who believe in God and in heaven, traditions or entertainment shape much of the popular understanding of heaven rather than biblical details of the heavenly realm.

Contemporary thinking has popularized the notion that heaven is not real. Existentialism reasons that the current reality is the only true reality, that nothing exists beyond this life, and that, therefore, life is meaningless. Atheism agrees that nothing awaits the end of the physical life. Atheism not only denies heaven but also the very idea of God. Darwinism closely relates to these ideologies, suggesting that humans were not created in the image of the eternal Creator God; instead, humans are merely a product of chance and evolutionary survival of the fittest. Ironically, Darwinism teaches the belief in perpetual improvement even while the world continues an unstopping course of corruption and decay.

In the beginning God created the heavens and the earth.

Genesis 1:1 NASB

The Spirit of God . . . puts a little of heaven in our hearts so that we'll never settle for less.

2 Corinthians 5:5 MSG

The biblical teaching of heaven is a distinct alternative to these baseless, hopeless philosophies. Because of heaven, people can understand that they were created in the image of God. Because of heaven, they can believe that Jesus came to rescue them from death. Because of heaven, humans have hope of restoration. Because of heaven, they can look forward to the life after death with an expectation of peace and blessing. Heaven is not just a possibility;

heaven is the assured reality for all those who would dare to believe in the promises of God. Jesus told his followers to look forward to heaven as a true, verifiable place that he would one day share with them forever.

Points to Remember

- Philosophies that deny the existence of God and the reality of heaven have no evidence in fact.

- Heaven is a real place revealed by God and promised by Jesus. The people who follow Jesus look forward to the place where they will be with him forever.

Check Your Understanding

- **What does it mean that to deny the reality of heaven is to deny the reality of God?**

It is impossible to separate belief in God from belief in heaven. If the Bible cannot be believed about its claims about heaven, it cannot be trusted about its claims about God. All the Bible's claims are trustworthy.

- **Why is it significant that Jesus spoke about heaven as a place he would share with others?**

The claim that Jesus will share heaven with people illustrates his purpose in coming to the earth to restore people to fellowship with God. It identifies heaven as a real place where people go after experiencing physical death.

FAQ–Where Is Heaven Located?

One difficulty for some people is their thinking that if heaven exists, then it should be a place that can be physically identified. In examining all the possible locations on the earth, no place matches the Bible's description. In exploring the firmament, no place has been identified by telescope or satellite that could even remotely be regarded as the dwelling place of God. The Bible speaks of heaven in celestial terms, but the human ability to locate it remains inadequate to the task.

Perhaps one reason why humans are frustrated in the effort to find heaven is that the Bible actually speaks of three locations, using the term *heaven* for each. The "first heaven" is simply the sky overhead. It is the earthly atmosphere dotted by clouds, moved by the winds, and filled with the earthly creatures of the skies. This atmosphere extends approximately seven miles into the sky.

The "second heaven" is the celestial heaven. This heaven is the universe and everything in it. The earth is part of it, as are the sun and its solar system, the Milky Way, and all the other galaxies. Scientists, despite continually improving technology, have been unable to number the stars or even the galaxies. Astronomical estimates count no fewer than seventy sextillion stars. Humans have not yet been able to locate the boundaries of the universe, and yet the second heaven is a finite creation of God.

The LORD looks from heaven. . . . From the place of His dwelling He looks on all the inhabitants of the earth.

Psalm 33:13–14 NKJV

Stephen was filled with the Holy Spirit. He looked toward heaven, where he saw our glorious God and Jesus standing at his right side.

Acts 7:55 CEV

The "third heaven" is the "heaven of heavens." It begins wherever the second heaven ends. The third heaven is God's home and where his throne is established. God fills this heaven with his presence. The third heaven is also the dwelling place of all the people who have been restored by God in the spiritual life. Virtually every reference to the third heaven is "up." In the Bible, Satan locates the third heaven above the stars. As impressive as it is, this heaven is temporary. One day, God will relocate it as part of his inauguration of the eternal heaven.

Points to Remember

- The heavens consist of the skies immediately overhead the earth as the "first heaven," the universe in all of its expanse as the "second heaven," and God's home as the "third heaven."

  - The location of the third heaven is beyond the unknown limit of the second heaven. The Bible declares it to be "up."

Check Your Understanding

- **Why is it important to understand the distinctions between the three heavens?**

It is important to distinguish between the three heavenly realms because it helps to understand where heaven may be located.

- **Why does it matter that heaven is "up"?**

It is important to know that the heaven of heavens is "up" because it indicates that heaven is not an earthly or universal realm. Heaven begins beyond the human ability to locate it, and it has no end.

FAQ—What Does It Mean to Praise God for Eternity?

The Jewish traditional wedding offers a provocative picture of heavenly events. The Bible illustrates that the setting of heaven will be like a wedding feast. Jesus is pictured as the groom, and the universal Christian community known as the church is pictured as the bride. The festive ceremony communicates the intimate union and deep, redemptive love that Jesus has for his people, who will be blessed to live forever in heaven with him. Heaven will be characterized by ongoing joy-filled celebrations honoring God's loving faithfulness.

In the Jewish tradition, the groom negotiates with the bride's father for his bride's dowry. Once the price is paid, the groom goes to his own father's house to build a home for his bride. At an unknown time, the groom returns with his groomsmen to a watchful bride and her bridal party. The marriage ceremony begins, the bride and groom are united, and the celebration follows. While the wedding guests feast and celebrate for seven days, the bride and groom are secluded in the marriage chamber. At the end of the seven days, the bride and groom join the guests.

This ancient tradition symbolizes the relationship between Jesus and his church. He is the groom, and the church is his bride. He redeemed the church by paying the "bride price" with his own life. Jesus went to heaven to prepare a place for every person within the church to live

Let us be glad and rejoice and give Him glory, for the marriage of the Lamb has come, and His wife has made herself ready.

Revelation 19:7 NKJV

The two shall become one flesh. This mystery is great; but I am speaking with reference to Christ and the church.

Ephesians 5:31–32 NASB

forever. The Bible promises that he will come at an unannounced time, claim the church, and be united with the church in heaven forever.

Every feast and commemorative celebration in the Bible is worth studying. Many theologians believe these feasts are not only historical, but also prophetic. This means that these ancient traditions will be fully understood and enjoyed in the context of heaven. The future of heaven promises to be filled with celebrations that testify to God's faithful love for people throughout and beyond all time, regardless of how it is measured.

Points to Remember

• The ancient Jewish festivals and commemorative celebrations are not only historical, but they are also prophetic. The marriage tradition shows a picture of Jesus' plan to welcome Christians to heaven.

• Every Christian should understand the promise of heaven as the fulfillment of a groom's commitment to his bride to love her perfectly and to give her the home he prepared for her.

Check Your Understanding

▪ **What is the significance of the symbolism of the traditional Jewish wedding to heaven?**

Just as the groom came and claimed the bride as he promised to do, Jesus has promised to claim those who follow him as Lord and take them to heaven with him.

▪ **What does it mean that festivals and commemorations are prophetic?**

The prophetic possibilities of biblical feasts and festivals means that the explicit instructions and details of these historic celebrations will be fully understood only when they are experienced in heaven in the fullness of time.

FAQ—Is Saint Peter the Doorman of the Pearly Gates?

"A guy goes to heaven where he's greeted at the Pearly Gates by Saint Peter." This opening line has introduced countless jokes over the years. The fact that many people have come to believe that heaven is a gated community and the apostle Peter serves as heaven's bouncer is no laughing matter. The Bible does speak about walls and gates that encompass the New Jerusalem of eternity, but much of what is commonly believed about the heavenly domain has no basis in Scripture. Likewise, the idea that Peter stands at a locked gate denying or granting entry hints to a nonbiblical understanding of what happens to a person who is granted entrance into heaven.

In eternity, the new earth will exist within the eternal heaven, and New Jerusalem will be the capital city. The Bible describes New Jerusalem as a city surrounded by walls that are fourteen hundred miles long, two hundred feet tall, and two hundred feet wide. The walls are constructed of jasper, a precious crystal that will perfectly reflect God's glory. The walls stand strong because of the twelve uniquely bejeweled foundations, each of which bears the name of a New Testament apostle. Each of the four walls contains three gates, and each gate is constructed from an immense single pearl. Each of the gates will be named after one of the twelve tribes of Israel.

> Each day its gates will never close because it will never be night there.
>
> Revelation 21:25 HCSB
>
> His master replied, "Well done, good and faithful servant! . . . Come and share your master's happiness!"
>
> Matthew 25:23 NIV

Most impressively, the Bible promises that the twelve gates of heaven will never close. The gates will remain open forever, allowing the residents of heaven to freely enter and depart from the city. The perpetually open gates also highlight the fact that heaven is a place of eternal peace. Even so, each gate is protected by a single angel, ever vigilant to watch and protect.

Finally, while the apostle Peter enjoys heaven along with all other citizens of God's eternal reward, Jesus alone grants entry into his presence. After the final judgment, Jesus will personally welcome each person to heaven, which will be a place of comfort and rest from the physical life of faith and toil.

Points to Remember

- Heaven has twelve open gates, each made from a single pearl, watched over by an angel.

- The apostle Peter will be honored in heaven with his name on a foundation of heaven's wall, but he is not heaven's gatekeeper.

- Jesus alone grants entry into heaven.

Check Your Understanding

- **Why isn't Peter at the gates of heaven?**

Peter is not at the gates of heaven because he, like all humans who receive the gift of heaven, is a citizen of heaven with a full, eternal life within and beyond its gates.

- **Why are the gates of heaven always open?**

The gates of heaven are always open because heaven is forever peaceful and its citizens will enjoy the freedom to explore the fullness of the heavenly realm. People will travel continually in and out of New Jerusalem.

FAQ—Do All Babies Get to Go to Heaven?

The pain of losing a baby to miscarriage or death in infancy or early childhood is overwhelming. Expectations are cut devastatingly short, and parents who were dreaming of their child's future suddenly must change their thinking to deal with the agonizing reality of their loss. Part of this naturally difficult process is asking questions about the spiritual destination of the child. Thankfully, the Bible offers hope to grieving loved ones and shows the depth of God's good nature and impeccable character.

⸭

The matter of what happens to the soul and spirit of a young child at death has challenged many people throughout history. Not only is the tragic situation understandably emotional, but it poses theological considerations that must be addressed. Ultimately, what matters is that people find the answers to this difficult question in the unchanging reliability of God's truth as recorded in the Bible.

Throughout the Scriptures, God has a high regard for children. King David recorded important understanding that demonstrates the depth of God's affection for the preborn and the newly born. King David wrote that every person is wonderfully made by God (Psalm 139:14). Other verses in this psalm explain that God knows beforehand every detail about every person's life, from the moment of creation to the moment of death. These verses indicate that God is intimately aware of his plans for every person before

Jesus . . . said to them, "Let the little children come to Me, and do not forbid them; for of such is the kingdom of God."

Mark 10:14 NKJV

At that time Jesus . . . said, "I praise you, Father, . . . because you have hidden these things from the wise and learned, and revealed them to little children."

Luke 10:21 NIV

that person is created. No person is created by accident, even if the birth seems to be unplanned according to human considerations. This means that in the sad times when a child dies, God foreknew the child's death and allowed it to happen.

That God would allow such an event might be difficult to understand, especially because the Bible presents God as loving and kind to the people whose faith is grounded in him. King David was certainly a person who could be described this way. Interestingly, his explanation of the full foreknowledge of God sprang from the deep pain of a personal tragedy. King David wrote these scriptural truths as a dad who had experienced the death of a newborn son.

The Bible tells that King David had a son with his wife Bathsheba. This child was sick for seven days, and for each of those days, David pleaded with God and refused to eat. On the seventh day, the child died. All the servants and respected leaders in David's household were concerned that David would react to news of his young son's death with an irrational, desperate response. David saw the servants whispering fearfully, so he asked them if his son had died. When they nervously acknowledged the tragedy, they were surprised by his response. He stood up, bathed, changed his clothes, and went to worship God. After his time of worship, he returned to his home and ate a meal.

King David's behavior baffled the servants. They asked him how he could be so composed immediately after such a disappointing response to a week of pleading with God. He told his servants that he pleaded with God while the child lived in hopes that his son would not die. He acknowledged that he did not know God's plan for his son. Now that his son had died, though, he could not change the circumstances. However, what David said next has given hope to grieving parents ever since.

He told his servants, "I will go to him, but he will not return to me" (2 Samuel 12:23 NIV). David took peace in knowing that God is merciful. God's grace is sufficient to overcome the flawed rebellious nature of the children who die too young to independently seek forgiveness.

David was confident that this same grace and mercy would facilitate his own eternal presence in heaven with God. At his son's death, he was similarly confident that one day he would be reunited in heaven with his son. While at some point each person becomes accountable to God for his individual decisions and will have to give account for any rebellion against God, the Bible promises that God offers a compensatory covering to children that ushers them into heaven for eternity when their brief physical lives end.

"Do you hear what these children are saying?" Jesus said, "Yes, I hear them. And haven't you read in God's Word, 'From the mouths of children and babies I'll furnish a place of praise'?"

Matthew 21:16 MSG

Myth Buster

In a well-known biblical passage, Jesus said, "I promise you this. If you don't change and become like a child, you will never get into the kingdom of heaven" (Matthew 18:3 CEV). Many people think this means that God requires every person to have a childlike faith to get into heaven. However, this means that God requires every person to have total dependence upon him—like a child—to get into heaven. Just as a child depends upon a parent for every physical need, so, too, does every person totally depend upon God for every spiritual need.

Points to Remember

- Unfortunately, a reality of physical life is that children sometimes die for any number of reasons. None of these deaths surprise God, even when the death is unexpected to the parents and family.

- God requires faith and belief for a person to go to heaven. A child is incapable of expressing these requirements, as far as humans are able to discern.

- The Bible indicates that young children are received into heaven because of their total dependence upon God and that parents with faith in God will be reunited with their children in heaven.

Check Your Understanding

- **What does it mean that every person is "wonderfully made"?**

God has prepared the life of every person according to his perfect plan, even when those details do not meet with human understanding or expectation.

- **Why did King David grieve while his son lived, but returned to his regular activity once his son died?**

David grieved while his son lived in the hope that his son's health would improve. When his son died, he returned to his regular activities because he understood that his faith in God promised a reunion with his son in heaven.

- **What is important for a parent to understand about the death of a child?**

Young children will be welcomed into heaven because of God's goodness. If a parent desires a reunion with his or her children in heaven, it is important that the parent have faith in God that will guarantee the reunion to occur.

FAQ—What Will We Eat and Drink in Heaven?

Most dieticians recommend that people eat three meals a day every day for maximum health. Too little food and people starve. Too much food and people experience risks of an entirely different sort. In heaven, people will have perfect bodies that will never get sick or die. The need for food in eternity seems superfluous, and yet there is no shortage of biblical anecdotes of both dining and drinking that will occur in heaven. The reasons for these meals give insight into the nature of the heavenly experience, and how those experiences will be enjoyed.

On earth, eating is a life-or-death matter. Unfortunately, eating has also been a continual source of disobedience, rebellion, and strife. God instituted dietary laws and encouraged people to be moderate in their consumption. The Bible explicitly warns against excessive food and drink. The fact that people struggle with rightly doing something as simple as eating and drinking illustrates the plight of the human in the physical life.

Here I am! I stand at the door and knock. If anyone hears my voice and opens the door, I will come in and eat with him, and he with me.

Revelation 3:20 NIV

I will freely give water from the life-giving fountain to everyone who is thirsty.

Revelation 21:6 CEV

However, the Bible also points to clear commands to share food and drink with others, and to faithfully practice hospitality. Some of Jesus' most provocative miracles involve food and drink. Jesus taught parables that compared the kingdom of God to a wedding feast, and the apostle John's prophecy of heaven similarly envisioned a large feast at an extravagant table filled with countless guests. The final invitations of Jesus to his followers are given in the imagery of eating and drinking.

One characteristic of heaven will be the prevalence of food and drink enjoyed in the company of God and other people. There will always be an abundance of it, and every person will enjoy it without the problems of greed, compulsion, or any other dysfunctional issue. Wine will be consumed in moderation without drunkenness, and meals will be enjoyed in the context of hospitality. No person will be in want or suffer from hunger or thirst, and every person in heaven will be invited to partake in the banquet hosted by God.

Points to Remember

- In the physical life, eating and drinking are matters of both necessity and personal struggle for many people. Neither of these matters will be a concern in heaven.

- In the physical life, eating and drinking are matters of both necessity and personal struggle for many people. Neither of these matters will be a concern in heaven.

- Heaven will be characterized by an abundance of hospitality and everlasting opportunities to have pleasant experiences with God and other people around the setting of food and drink.

Check Your Understanding

▪ Why won't eating be a necessity in heaven?

Eating will not be a necessity in heaven because the eternal bodies that God provides are incorruptible. This means they cannot weaken, get ill, grow weary, or die.

▪ If eating is unnecessary in heaven, why will people do it?

God determined that food is good and pleasing. He gives food as a blessing to be enjoyed with loved ones, and heaven offers this blessing as part of the hospitality and relationship experience of heaven.

God—Describing the Indescribable Host of Heaven

When the apostle John saw God in heaven, the sight was too overwhelming to describe. In heaven, God reveals himself fully to people, and everyone will understand the mysteries of the Creator.

Contents

God in Heaven—The Fatherly King 113

Jesus in Heaven—The Heavenly Responsibilities of
the Son of God 115

The Holy Spirit in Heaven—The Counseling
Creator in Eternity 119

The Eternal Word of God—The Role of the Bible
in Heaven 121

FAQ—What Will It Mean to See God in Heaven? 123

FAQ—How Will God Rule in Eternity? 125

FAQ—How Will God Relate to His Creation in Eternity? 127

FAQ—What Are the Names of God in Heaven? 131

Dear friends, now we are children of God, and what we will be has not yet been made known. But we know that when he appears, we shall be like him, for we shall see him as he is.

1 John 3:2 NIV

God in Heaven—The Fatherly King

Throughout the New Testament, God is described as "Father." He is the Father of creation, the Father of Israel, the Father of Jesus, the Father of the Gentiles, and the Father of all people. Though God is Spirit and is neither expressly male nor female, he is ascribed primarily masculine characteristics exemplified in his role as Father. The fatherhood of God helps people understand that he created humans for eternal relationship in a familial manner. Nowhere will this understanding be better and more fully understood than when humans in heaven encounter their heavenly Father face-to-face.

In the Old Testament, the prophets and psalmists identified God as "Father." They showed God as a caring disciplinarian and Redeemer by means of a personal faith relationship. This concept was radical and revolutionary. Prior to this revelation, other religions believed God was unknowable and difficult to please.

In love he predestined us to be adopted as his sons through Jesus Christ, in accordance with his pleasure and will.

Ephesians 1:4–5 NIV

We know, dear brothers and sisters, that God loves you and has chosen you to be his own people.

1 Thessalonians 1:4 NLT

With the advent of Jesus, the fatherhood of God was understood even more. Jesus presented God as the Father who knows every detail of every person's life. He is the heavenly Father, who willingly did everything necessary to rescue his children from the pains of hell. God the heavenly Father is the equal collaborator in redemption with Jesus. He is the Father of compassion and Lord over his heavenly family.

Because of God's fatherhood in heaven, people are able to relate to him as his children. They can stake claim to his inheritance, which is understood to be the kingdom of heaven and all its rights, responsibilities, and opportunities. Furthermore, people who go to heaven are blessed as the adopted, chosen children of God. This means that no person's salvation was accidental, circumstantial, or in any way coincidental. God deliberately chose to exercise the forgiveness that is required to welcome a formerly rebellious individual into his own family. In the physical reality here on earth, that relationship is understood by faith. In the spiritual eternity, redeemed humans will experience that relationship fully.

Points to Remember

• God is Spirit and is neither male nor female. However, God relates to humans as Father. He chose to interact with people this way as an expression of his loving desire to have a relationship with people in terms they could understand and appreciate.

• Humans in heaven will enjoy relationship with God as his adopted children. They will have access to all of God's possessions as his adopted children and the inheritors to all that is his.

Check Your Understanding

▪ Why is it significant that God identifies himself as "Father" to people who respond to him by faith?

God's fatherhood is significant because it means God can be known and that people can relate to God both in the physical life by faith and in the spiritual life face-to-face.

▪ Why does it matter that God has adopted those who follow him by faith?

God's adoption means that every person has an equal opportunity to have a relationship with God and that every adopted child of God in heaven enjoys all the rights and privileges afforded to him as such.

Jesus in Heaven—The Heavenly Responsibilities of the Son of God

Jesus is likely the most enigmatic personality in all religious thought. No figure is more disputed, and virtually every world religion has a theological position on who Jesus was and what he did and did not accomplish. He is a polarizing figure and has been considered a prophet, a priest, a king, a teacher, a reincarnated ancient personality, a good example, a radical revolutionary, the Messiah. Despite all this confusion, Jesus himself was never confused or ambiguous about his identity. As such, his role in future events is determined and his role as eternal Lord is biblically indisputable.

Jesus is one part of the triune God—three in one. He is God, and, at the same time, he is the Son of God. He was present and active in the creation of the universe. He was witness to the expulsion of Lucifer from the highest heaven. He was present at every age and has served as captain of his heavenly army throughout the generations. He periodically has visited Old Testament personalities, and he foretold his own coming. He is described as the "Beginning," the "Alpha," and the "Word" that was "in the beginning." He is the Light of the World and the hope of all humanity.

For this reason the Father loves Me, because I lay down My life so that I may take it again.

John 10:17 NASB

Then I saw Heaven open wide—and oh! a white horse and its Rider. The Rider, named Faithful and True, judges and makes war in pure righteousness.

Revelation 19:11 MSG

The Bible tells that Jesus reigned over creation from his throne in heaven as God, but he willfully stepped out of his heavenly robe and entered into time and humanity as a baby. Jesus was born as a baby and took on the human form. He lived a life of perfect obedience to the Father, and he was totally without sin. He was the only person able to do this, even though he faced every sort of temptation that is common to humans. He fulfilled numerous prophecies about the Messiah as a demonstration of his divine identity, and he performed a multitude of miracles to demonstrate his power over the entire world—life, death, and disobedience itself. Eventually, Jesus completed his work of redemption by dying on the cross at the hands of his Jewish and Gentile accusers. In doing so, Jesus satisfied the wrath of God against all human rebellion. He bought back his people by paying the ransom and freeing them from the penalty of sin.

He did this as part of his own plan to redeem humans who were separated from God because of their disobedient rebellion. Jesus himself overcame death. In doing so, he made heaven and eternal life a reality for all people who would trust that this effort was satisfactory and successful. When Jesus did this, he completed the plan that he established before he initiated time. Jesus accomplished his plan, which was the first step in the total redemption of all that was corrupted through the disobedience of humans and satanic rebellion.

Although making heaven available to people is a significant work in the plan of Jesus, it is only one of his responsibilities, as detailed in the Bible. The Bible declares that Jesus still has much to do prior to the establishment of the permanent heaven. Between now and then, Jesus must claim all Christians as belonging to him. He will return to the earth and rule it along with his faithful human followers for one thousand years. Following this time, Jesus will lead a final battle against Satan and the fallen angel's rebellious forces. After his final defeat of Satan, Jesus will sit as Judge in a series of judgments. First, he will judge the present earth as cursed and destroy it by fire. Then, he will judge Christians and give them rewards for their faith. Finally, Jesus will judge nonbelievers by the works of their lives and assign them to hell alongside Satan.

After Jesus concludes his plan of redemption, he will inaugurate the onset of eternity. Jesus will cast death and hades, the temporary hell, into the

I am Jesus! And I am the one who sent my angel to tell all of you these things for the churches. I am David's Great Descendant, and I am also the bright morning star.

Revelation 22:16 CEV

lake of fire, the permanent home of tormenting judgment against disobedience. Jesus will then introduce the unified heaven and earth through the New Jerusalem and dwell there with redeemed humans forever.

In the eternal heaven, Jesus will reign as King. He will be the light of eternity, and he will fill it with his presence. He will be worshiped as he reigns with total authority from his heavenly throne.

Digging Deeper

Some people consider God cruel for sentencing Jesus to death on a cross. It is utterly incomprehensible that a loving God could permit or ordain such a barbaric act. However, Jesus was never forced or coerced into this sacrifice. Jesus declared that he willingly gave up his life. He predicted his own death multiple times prior to its occurring. The reality is, Jesus voluntarily left the throne of heaven. He knew he would be born to die so that all people who believe could live forever in heaven with him.

Points to Remember

- Jesus was a coequal collaborator with God the Father in the plan to redeem humans. He fully participated. In this cooperative effort, Jesus demonstrated that he is equally God in every way.

• Jesus still must return to the earth, claim the final victory over Satan, judge humanity, and reign over heaven forever. Just as he has fulfilled all promises related to his first time on the earth, he will complete all these future works as promised as well.

Check Your Understanding

▪ **What is significant about the multiple roles of Jesus throughout history?**

The multiple responsibilities of Jesus throughout and beyond history demonstrate that Jesus is God.

▪ **Why does it matter that Jesus voluntarily gave up his life on the cross?**

Jesus' voluntary death on the cross shows that Jesus was not a forced sacrifice and that he collaborated in God's redemptive plan.

▪ **What happened when Jesus overcame death?**

When Jesus overcame death, he made heaven and eternal life a reality for all people who would trust that this effort was satisfactory and successful.

▪ **Who do other religions say Jesus was?**

Nearly every world religion has a theological position on who Jesus was and what he did and did not accomplish. He has been considered a prophet, a priest, a king, a teacher, a reincarnated ancient personality, a good example, a radical revolutionary, and the Messiah.

The Holy Spirit in Heaven—
The Counseling Creator in Eternity

The Holy Spirit is often the forgotten aspect of the triune Godhead. Perhaps this is so because the Holy Spirit is not emphasized in Old Testament activity, or because the Holy Spirit was promised to come only after Jesus was resurrected. Many people mistakenly believe that the Holy Spirit has limited responsibilities and that he will one day no longer be needed. However, God's Holy Spirit, like the Father and Son, is eternal and everlasting. He will be present in heaven forever, and the fullness of the Godhead will be complete eternally.

The Holy Spirit was present in the beginning, hovering over the waters of the formless expanse before the universe's creation. He was also a collaborator in creation. The image of the Holy Spirit is reflected in the human spirit. God's Holy Spirit visited the earth many times in biblical history and was the promised helper spoken of by Jesus. The Holy Spirit came as promised at Pentecost and has been with believers ever since. He actively leads, encourages, exhorts, and convicts followers of Christ every day across the world.

In future political, social, and spiritual upheavals, the Holy Spirit will be vigilant in leading many people to believe in Jesus as Messiah. He will empower converts to Christianity to perform supernatural acts, just as he did in Old Testament times. As Jesus reigns on the earth for one thousand years, the Holy Spirit will be active in helping people live

The Spirit of the LORD shall rest upon Him, the Spirit of wisdom and understanding, the Spirit of counsel and might, the Spirit of knowledge and of the fear of the LORD.

Isaiah 11:2 NKJV

There is one body and one Spirit, just as you were called to one hope at your calling.

Ephesians 4:4 HCSB

holy lives. The Bible declares that Jesus will rule with the Holy Spirit's wisdom, insight, and understanding.

The Holy Spirit is symbolized in heaven as the seven spirits of perfection before the throne of God. God's Holy Spirit is the church's helper that protected, unified, and blessed the kingdom of God on earth, and secured it until it could be redeemed in heaven. The Holy Spirit is the eternal God, and he will be fully understood and worshiped in heaven.

Points to Remember

• The Holy Spirit is eternal. He is God, present at creation and in history. He can be observed as active in both the Old and the New Testaments and is represented in prophecies about eternity.

• The Holy Spirit has future responsibilities that he will fulfill, and he will be present in heaven alongside the Father and the Son.

• The Holy Spirit is God himself and not merely a tool or resource of God.

Check Your Understanding

• **Why does it matter that the Holy Spirit is eternal?**

The Holy Spirit had, has, and will have essential responsibilities to fulfill in the work of human redemption and eternal rule.

• **What does it mean that the Holy Spirit is the helper?**

The role of the Holy Spirit as helper means that he leads people to faith in Jesus and offers the hope of forgiveness and of eternal life in heaven.

The Eternal Word of God—
The Role of the Bible in Heaven

The fourth Gospel, the Gospel of John, declares that the Bible is the written account of the life of Jesus Christ. This means that the written words are eternal and that the role the Bible fulfills in heaven is more than prophecy, more than narrative, more than mere story. The words and promises written in the Bible—the words of God—are the foundation of Christian belief about heaven, and every promise will be fulfilled in heaven.

The Bible is sometimes called God's Word or the Word of God. This is more than description. It is a revelation of Jesus. If you know the content and message of the Bible, then you can know Jesus experientially. That is, you can experience Jesus in your heart and in your life. Jesus declared during his earthly ministry that he did not intend to invalidate the words of the Old Testament; rather, he came to fulfill the Old Testament and give it fullness of meaning. Jesus is the fulfillment of prophecy.

Everything about the everlasting reality in heaven agrees with and is in accord with the Bible's promises. Nothing in heaven will disagree with any biblical detail. In fact, in the full disclosure of heaven, all of the details that seem obscure,

> Assuredly, I say to you, till heaven and earth pass away, one jot or one tittle will by no means pass from the law till all is fulfilled.
>
> Matthew 5:18 NKJV
>
> The rider wore a robe that was covered with blood, and he was known as "The Word of God."
>
> Revelation 19:13 CEV

confusing, difficult, or unclear will be illuminated for understanding. Jesus even said that he came to establish every "jot and tittle" of the Scriptures. This means that the life of Jesus and his reign in heaven will allow for an accurate understanding of every passage, verse, sentence, word, punctuation, and even the spaces between words and letters. In heaven, it will be understood that God is in even the smallest of biblical details.

Points to Remember

• "Word of God" underscores the significance of the Bible's relationship with eternity. The Bible reveals the truth about Jesus. Everything that needs to be known about Jesus can be known by reading what the Bible says about him.

• Jesus explained that one of his purposes was to fulfill, or to make real, every detail of the Bible. This will be fully understood only in the context of eternity.

Check Your Understanding

▪ **What is significant about Jesus' statement that he came to fulfill "every jot and tittle" of the Scriptures?**

This statement is significant because it reveals that Jesus is sovereign over every detail of the Bible. Even the spaces between letters and words have significance that will be understood only as Jesus reveals it in heaven.

▪ **What does it mean that the Bible is foundational in heaven?**

This concept means that the Word of God—God's truth and reality communicated in the Bible—reveals the intrinsic substance of heaven. Everything claimed in the Bible is made real in heaven.

FAQ—What Will It Mean to See God in Heaven?

The heavenly experience is only partially understood while a person remains in the living realm. The Bible describes it as looking through a dark glass. However, some of the details in the biblical text should whet the interests of every person. Heaven promises unique experiences with God and thrilling adventures of the grandest scale. God has ordained that his children collaborate with him in the culmination of global events, in the transition into eternity, and in the life everlasting.

While the Bible dispels myths about heaven, perhaps the most important notion that the Bible refutes is the idea that heaven will be boring. Boring? Nothing could be further from the truth. The reality is that the citizens of heaven will have a vigorous, active, and highly interactive life. Particularly relevant is the involvement of heaven's residents in end-times affairs. The Bible speaks of a time when people who come to faith immediately prior to Christ's return will be killed for their faith.

> I saw underneath the altar the souls of those who had been slain because of the word of God . . . and they cried out with a loud voice.
>
> Revelation 6:9–10 NASB

> The armies in heaven, clothed in fine linen, white and clean, followed Him on white horses.
>
> Revelation 19:14 NKJV

As these martyrs are ushered into heaven, they will join a heavenly assembly that calls upon Jesus to judge the earth. They will not be calling for revenge, however; they will be asking God to exercise his might and establish his holy kingdom on earth. The Bible says that God will honor this petition of the people by engaging in the final conquest of and victory over Satan and his collaborators.

All of heaven will rejoice and worship Jesus. Jesus will head a royal family that includes all the citizenry of the heavenly domain. Jesus will know each one of heaven's occupants, and each person in heaven will know Jesus in a full, physical, and personal understanding.

Points to Remember

- Heaven is more than "going to a better place." It is about fully relating to and interacting with God.

- God determined that people would be actively involved in the events that lead to the end of time, as well as in the time of eternity that follows. Humans will both oppose and support God.

Check Your Understanding

- **Why does it matter that heaven is an interactive environment?**

The interactivity of heaven is significant because it reveals that heaven will be an exciting place with more to do than a person can begin to comprehend.

- **What is significant about the types of actions God will initiate in heaven?**

Heaven is not simply a place of adventure; it is from heaven that God will launch his final offensive against disobedience and rebellion, and he has chosen to include people in the work of that victory.

FAQ—How Will God Rule in Eternity?

Jesus taught his followers to pray, asking God every day that his kingdom will come and that he will rule on the earth the same way he rules in heaven. The current administration of the earth is completely unlike the reign of God in heaven. Furthermore, since it would be senseless for Jesus to lead his followers to pray a prayer that God could not or would not answer, it makes sense that at some point in the future, God's reign upon the earth will look the same as it does in heaven.

The Bible speaks to a time when Jesus will rule upon the earth for a thousand years. This thousand-year period will be marked by unprecedented peace and prosperity. Satan will be bound in hell during this time, and the world will not know of any war or upheaval. However, at the end of the thousand years, Satan will be released for a final time of spiritual rebellion. Satan will gather many rebellious people to war against Jesus, but Jesus will ultimately and swiftly defeat them all. This final victory will mark the beginning of the final judgment and the inauguration of the eternal heaven and hell.

> The LORD reigns, He is clothed with majesty; the LORD is clothed, He has girded Himself with strength. Surely the world is established, so that it cannot be moved.
>
> Psalm 93:1 NKJV
>
> He will rule them with an iron scepter.
>
> Revelation 19:15 NIV

In the permanent heaven, God will rule from his throne in the New Jerusalem. God and humankind will dwell together in joy and true happiness in the unified heaven and earth. His rule will be a benevolent monarchy, a gift of kindness and love to his people. His reign will also be a theocracy because all creation will worship him as Lord. No faith will be needed for this worship because faith will have already been proven justified.

God's reign will be without equal and without end as he rules with perfect love and perfect holiness.

Points to Remember

- God's rule in the future will be marked by the reign of Jesus for a thousand years on earth before the final battle against Satan. The thousand years will be an unprecedented time of peace and harmony that will be upset at its conclusion by a final rebellion, in which Jesus will defeat Satan.

- After Satan's final rebellion is crushed, God will unite the new heaven, the new earth, and the New Jerusalem, and he will reign perfectly from this new location forever.

Check Your Understanding

- **Why will Satan be released at the end of the thousand years?**

Satan will be released after a thousand years for a time of final rebellion. Jesus will overcome this rebellion and use the victory to launch eternity.

- **What does it mean that Jesus will reign during this unprecedented era of peace?**

Jesus will reign during this time with an iron scepter. He will rule with perfect holiness and wisdom and will reign as the Messiah.

FAQ—How Will God Relate to His Creation in Eternity?

The Bible defines faith as the spiritual substance of what a person hopes for in God. This faith is based on the unseen evidence of personal experience. This means that people have personal experiences that help them relate to God. These experiences become the bedrock on which future faith is built. For all the experiences required to build and add to faith in life, it seems unexplainable that faith is unnecessary in heaven. There will be no faith in heaven. Everything that was unseen in the physical life will be visible in the eternal life. Everything that was hoped for will be realized. Eternity will be unlike anything ever experienced in the physical realm.

In this physical life, Christians relate to God exclusively by faith. From salvation to every experience that follows it, the Christian life requires some measure of faith to be added to whatever knowledge, wisdom, insight, or understanding a person has with regard to spiritual experience. Real faith is based on unseen evidence.

The promise of eternity is that all faith will be fulfilled and that all hopes and expectations will indeed be realized. The Bible says that every person will finally encounter God as he truly is. The apostle John wrote about his own prophetic encounter in symbolic terms. In those passages, Jesus is presented

If your work passes inspection, fine; if it doesn't, your part of the building will be torn out and started over. But you won't be torn out; you'll survive.

1 Corinthians 3:14–15 MSG

I no longer call you slaves. . . . Now you are my friends, since I have told you everything the Father told me.

John 15:15 NLT

as the Lion of Judah; the slain Lamb; the rider of a white horse; the Judge of the earth's churches with eyes of fire, feet of brass, and a thundering voice. He is the only one worthy to open the seals of God's judgments upon the earth. He is the one who holds the keys to heaven as well as to hell. He will lead the final battle with the sword of God's Word issuing forth from his own mouth. He will be seated upon the throne of God, and he will reign in heaven forever. The very image of Jesus caused John to fall upon his face as though dead!

God's reign in heaven will be marked by his deliberate interaction with his creation. In the end-times events that will precede the onset of eternity, the souls of people martyred for their faith will speak directly to Jesus, asking him not to delay his judgment upon evil any longer. Attending angels will praise Jesus and extol his glory, blessings, wisdom, thanksgiving, honor, power, and might. Jesus' perfection will be magnified to all of heaven forever.

The final judgment for Christians in heaven will be the rewards judgment, which is a judgment of rewards for those who followed Jesus by faith in the physical life. It will be a one-on-one experience with Jesus Christ where he assesses every deed done by every individual. This time will not be without tears and regret. Anything that God judges as having been done apart from faith will be judged as useless and forbidden in heaven. This will likely be a time of significant regret and profound awareness of lost opportunities. However, the Bible says that every person will receive commendation of some sort. God will wipe away every tear following the judgment, and every activity done in life as a response to faith will be commended and rewarded.

God's promise to the residents of heaven is to give them a home that surpasses their most creative imaginings. He promises to give them access to all the resources of heaven, because he has identified them as his heirs. He promises to reward them for their obedience and to bring them perfect peace and complete joy.

All who win the victory will be given these blessings. I will be their God, and they will be my people.

Revelation 21:7 CEV

The people of heaven will dwell with God and interact with him face-to-face, and they will dine with him, worship him as Lord, and relate with him as friend, Father, and as the Almighty. They will serve God with complete joy, living forever in the unmatched light of his perfect glory.

Myth Buster

The inheritance awaiting the followers of Christ is unlike the inheritance experienced in the earthly realm. The Bible says that anyone whose name is written in the Book of Life has overcome the physical life and the pain of death. These overcomers will be known as God's children, and they will inherit all things. This means that all the blessings of heaven are afforded to all the people who enter it.

Points to Remember

- There is no faith in heaven because there will be no need for faith there. In heaven, the faith of the physical life will be fulfilled and realized.

- God will relate fully with his creation as Master, Lord, Father, and friend. In heaven, God will be fully understood and experienced.

- People will receive a full inheritance from God and blessings for the faith that they exercised and developed during the physical life.

Check Your Understanding

- **What does it mean that every citizen of heaven will inherit all things?**

A citizen of heaven's "full inheritance" means that God will withhold nothing from any person who will call heaven home. People will interact with God in his fullness, and they will experience heaven to their capacity for doing so as demonstrated in the physical life.

- **Why will people shed tears at the rewards judgment where rewards are given?**

People will express regret and remorse as every deed is assessed and judged. Any deed not worthy of reward will be judged and burned, causing regret over lost opportunities.

- **Why is it significant that there will be no faith in heaven?**

The absence of faith in heaven means that every hope, every expectation, and every promise from God has been fulfilled and realized in the context of eternity.

- **How is faith defined?**

The Bible defines faith as the spiritual substance of what a person hopes for in God. This faith is based on the unseen evidence of personal experience.

FAQ—What Are the Names of God in Heaven?

Throughout history, God has been known by numerous titles and descriptions. Typically, these names have been indicative of his nature, his characteristics, or the qualities relevant to the particular circumstance where the respective name was used. In this inspiring tradition, much was revealed about God's goodness and love. His names demonstrated might, power, care, and concern. God will reveal even more about himself in heaven as he permits himself to be fully known by his adopted children.

Some of the names of God—Father, Son, Holy Spirit—expressed in heaven include:

Almighty. He is all-knowing, all-powerful, and ever-present.

Alpha and Omega; Beginning and End; First and Last. He is the author, sustainer, and conclusion of every detail of human history.

Amen. Everything Jesus does is in agreement with the will of the Father.

Beginning of the Creation of God. Jesus is co-creator with the Father and is his only begotten Son.

Bridegroom. Jesus will love the people of faith as a perfect husband loves his own bride.

Bright and Morning Star. Jesus is the source of all love, light, truth, hope, joy, holiness, and righteousness.

For this reason God also highly exalted Him and gave Him the name that is above every name.

Philippians 2:9 HCSB

His eyes are a flame of fire, and on His head are many diadems; and He has a name written on Him which no one knows except Himself.

Revelation 19:12 NASB

Christ. Jesus is the Messiah of God, promised to deliver all people and reign forever as Lord.

Faithful and True Witness. Everything Jesus did was an accurate reflection of the will and way of the Father.

Faithful Witness. Jesus faithfully and accurately spoke of the coming kingdom of God.

Firstborn from the Dead. Jesus is the only begotten Son of God.

He Who Has the Sharp Two-Edged Sword. All of God's Word is understood fully only in the context of Jesus.

He Who Holds the Key of David, Lion of the Tribe of Judah, the Root of David. Jesus is the rightful heir of Israel's throne.

He Who Holds the Seven Stars in His Right Hand, Who Walks in the Midst of the Seven Golden Lampstands. Jesus is the Judge over the churches, assessing and receiving the worship of history's believers.

He Who Is Holy, He Who Is True. Jesus alone is perfect and without sin. He is the fullness of truth.

He Who Lives, and Was Dead, and Is Alive Forevermore. Jesus affirms the validity of his own life, death, and resurrection as the means by which people experience the resurrected life with God after death.

He Who Opens and No One Shuts, and Shuts and No One Opens. God is always in total control. Nothing can circumvent or overcome his will.

He Who Sat on the Cloud. Another picture of Jesus' sovereignty, here in the context of impending judgment of wrath upon sin and rebellion.

He Who Sat on the Great White Throne. God is the Judge of all nonbelievers.

He Who Sat on the Horse. Jesus is the leader of his military.

He Who Was and Is and Is to Come. Jesus is eternal, forever existing in past, present, and future.

Her Child. Jesus was born to the people of Israel. He loves Israel and will redeem the people of Israel.

I Am. God recalls his own name spoken to Moses. He is the God of every current moment.

Lamb as Though It Had Been Slain. Jesus is God's worthy and satisfactory sacrifice for the sins of all heaven's citizens.

Lord God of the Holy Prophets. Jesus is the Lord over the prophets who foretold his birth, life, death and resurrection.

> Glorify the LORD with me; let us exalt his name together.
>
> Psalm 34:3 NIV

Lord God Omnipotent. God is all-powerful.

Lord of Lords and King of Kings. Nobody is sovereign over Jesus.

Lord, He Who Sits on the Throne. God reigns in heaven as King.

Ruler over the Kings of the Earth. Jesus is the Lord of all the earth's rulers.

Seven Spirits. He is the Holy Spirit of perfection with all the divine attributes of God.

Son of God. Jesus is divine. He possesses all of God's attributes, and he is fit to judge and reign.

Son of Man. Jesus was born fully human, born to serve all humanity, and born to die so that all people could live forever in eternity.

Word of God. Again, Jesus is the living embodiment of the Scriptures.

Digging Deeper

How God can be known in heaven is revealed by how he is presented in the Bible. As impressive and comprehensive as these descriptions are, the most provocative aspect is one that is scarcely mentioned in the Bible and is as-yet unrevealed in meaning. The Bible reveals that Jesus has a name that no one but himself knows. Names are important to God. A name is not just a description; it is a marker of one's true nature and character. The revelation of God's unknown name promises to be a glorious event!

Points to Remember

- The names of God reveal different aspects of his nature and character. These names show his might, his royalty, his protection, his love, and his authority over time and creation. The multitude of his names also reveals the depth of his complexity and the vastness of his divinity.

- The multitude of names used to address Jesus in heaven demonstrates his comprehensive involvement and authority over every detail of eternity.

Check Your Understanding

- **What does it mean that Jesus is the Bright and Morning Star?**

This title means that the holiness and purity of Jesus is the source of light for eternity.

- **Why is it important to know and understand the names of God?**

By knowing and understanding the names of God, a person better knows and understands God himself.

- **What does it mean that Jesus is Christ?**

The title Christ means that Jesus is the one anointed by God and appointed by God to carry out God's plan for redeeming human beings. Jesus alone bears the title Christ.

Angels—God's Messengers

Apart from humans, angels are perhaps God's most important
creation in carrying out his plan leading toward eternity.
Separate the legends from the legitimacy in what the
Bible reveals about these heavenly messengers.

Contents

Instant Messaging, Invincible Military—
The Responsibilities of Angels 137

The Named Angels—Meet God's Most Famous
Messengers 139

Historic Angelic Battles and What You Can Know
from Them.. 141

The Role of Fallen Angels in Temptation, Possession,
and Sin... 143

FAQ—What Is the Role of Angels in a Person's Death? 147

FAQ—How Do You Relate to Angelic Beings in This Life?.... 149

FAQ—How Will You Relate to Angels in Eternity? 153

FAQ—Are Angels Really People with Wings? 155

FAQ—When Did God Create Angels? 159

FAQ—What Are the Limitations of Angels? 163

I assure you . . . a messenger is not greater
than the one who sent him.

John 13:16 HCSB

Instant Messaging, Invincible Military—
The Responsibilities of Angels

Angels are provocative creatures who have been given consistent responsibilities throughout history. These duties have required regular interaction throughout history, and the promises of future events show that these dealings among and at times against humans will not change. In fact, the work that angels do in obedience to God will play an essential part in God's plan to bring history to a close and usher in eternity. In understanding the work of angels, it is possible to gain insight about how God created even angels with humans in mind.

✳

The main responsibility of angels is to serve as God's messengers. They interact periodically with humans to communicate important truths regarding God's plans. These plans typically concern the rescue of people, God's judgment, or a revelatory announcement. Angels warned Abraham of Sodom and Gomorrah's impending destruction. An angel told Mary that she would bear the child who was the Christ. An angel visited Joseph in his dreams and affirmed the news of Mary's divinely inspired pregnancy. An angel met Mary Magdalene at Jesus' tomb to tell her that he had risen from the dead.

> Because you have made the LORD . . . your dwelling place . . . He will give His angels orders concerning you, to protect you in all your ways.
>
> Psalm 91:9–11 HCSB
>
> Are not all angels ministering spirits sent to serve those who will inherit salvation?
>
> Hebrews 1:14 NIV

Angels also serve as God's military. The same two angels who rescued Lot from the evil men of Sodom and Gomorrah destroyed the cities shortly thereafter. The Bible reports that a single angel destroyed the Assyrian army, which numbered 185,000 men, while they slept, because the Assyrian king dared to overthrow Jerusalem. Angels will also be responsible for sorting the humans who will not go to heaven from those who will.

Finally, angels are ministering spirits. This means they tend to the physical, emotional, and spiritual needs of those to whom they are sent. Jesus received their ministry after withstanding the temptation of Satan. The angels also strengthened him to endure the torture he would receive on the cross. Furthermore, God assigns angels to protect the people who have sought to find the refuge for their needs in him through faith. God's angels do his bidding, without reservation and in total obedience and service to him.

Points to Remember

- Angels are God's messengers. They communicate messages that God wants people to know.

- Angels are God's military. They fight against God's enemies as he commands.

- Angels are God's ministering spirits. They tend to the needs of those whom God loves.

Check Your Understanding

- **What does it mean that angels are "ministering spirits"?**

When angels serve as ministering spirits, they function as agents of God's goodness toward people who trust him by faith. These angels will at times meet the physical, emotional, and spiritual needs of those to whom they are sent.

- **Why is the military service of angels significant?**

The military service of angels is significant because it reveals that God cares enough about his holiness to employ a force of angels to ensure that judgment will be executed according to his standards. He will not let evil and ungodliness go unaddressed.

The Named Angels—
Meet God's Most Famous Messengers

Around the world and from time immemorial, authors have created tales, myths, and legends relating the exploits of many angels. As in any good saga, these characters have been named and characterized in detail to explain their heroic or notorious deeds. Despite the exploits of these fictionalized creatures found throughout history, the Bible names only three angels. Unlike the imaginary angels that were based upon them, the trio of angels named in the Bible are indeed real and have contributed vitally to the advance of history and the work of God's plan for humans.

Of the three named angels, the notorious "Lucifer" mentioned in Isaiah 14:12 is commonly understood to be the fallen angel today known as Satan. However, the validity of his original name is disputed, since the word *Lucifer* is a Latin word used in a fourth-century translation of the original Hebrew texts. Elsewhere in the same Latin translation, *Lucifer* is also used to describe Jesus as the Morning Star (2 Peter 1:19). While it is unclear at best if the fallen angel's name was actually Lucifer, it is clear that today he is rightly named Satan, as the adversary of both God and humans.

The name of the angel Gabriel, however, is undisputed. He is the clarion of God, sent to offer announcements and proclamations to people throughout history. Gabriel is mentioned by name in both the Old and the New Testaments. Gabriel

War broke out in Heaven. Michael and his Angels fought the Dragon. The Dragon and his Angels fought back, but were no match for Michael.

Revelation 12:7–8 MSG

The angel said, "I am Gabriel! I stand in the very presence of God. It was he who sent me to bring you this good news!"

Luke 1:19 NLT

visited Daniel and interpreted an important prophetic dream for him. Centuries later, Gabriel announced to Mary that she would miraculously become pregnant with the promised Christ.

Likewise, the angel Michael is named in both the Old and the New Testaments. However, while Gabriel was God's messenger, Michael is God's soldier. He served Daniel by fighting those who opposed the Persian king Darius. In the New Testament, Michael is revealed to have contended with Satan for the body of Moses, and is named in the book of Revelation for warring against Satan. While all angels are likely named, these identified angels show that the real attention belongs focused on the work of God.

Points to Remember

• The identities of only two of the three named angels are explicitly known; the third named angel, Lucifer, has traditionally been identified as Satan.

• More important than angels' names are the deeds they perform in serving God. Gabriel is known to announce God's messages, and Michael is known to fight in behalf of God's causes.

Check Your Understanding

▪ **What is important to remember about the name of Satan?**

The validity of Satan's original name as "Lucifer" is disputed. However, his title Satan as the adversary of God and humans is not disputed. His original name is not important, but his role in deceiving people is essential to remember.

▪ **What is the significance of the angels in the Bible being named?**

Though the names of the angels are infrequent, they are consistently presented with specific responsibilities. This shows that angels have specific tasks to perform according to God's design.

Historic Angelic Battles and What You Can Know from Them

At various times in history, God's angels have participated in important battles in the realms of both heaven and earth. They have warred among themselves, and they have been used as instruments of judgment against humans. These battles have demonstrated the awe-inspiring might of angels, as well as the overwhelming power of God that is behind the power of the angelic forces. These conflicts not only have been a part of the past, but they also give insight to the promise of future conflicts, in which the Bible foretells additional angelic involvement.

God has used angels as instruments of judgment against humans, often with devastating results. Two angels entered Sodom and Gomorrah and brought destruction upon their population because of rampant rebellion against God's laws. Much later, Israel's king Hezekiah was distressed as Assyria's armies advanced toward Israel, intending to overthrow Hezekiah and establish their own pagan rule. That night, God sent a single angel who slew 185,000 Assyrians. This caused the Assyrian king to retreat to Nineveh, where he was killed by his own sons.

> The LORD sent an angel to the camp of the Assyrians, and he killed one hundred eighty-five thousand of them.
>
> Isaiah 37:36 CEV
>
> Bless GOD, all you armies of angels, alert to respond to whatever he wills.
>
> Psalm 103:21 MSG

Angels war not only against evil humans, but also against evil angels. The Bible speaks about a past heavenly war where a third of all angels joined Satan in his rebellion. God cast all the revolting angels from heaven and confined them to the universal domain. Another similar battle will occur in the future, with the same victorious results of God's obedient angels. God consistently brings victory to his faithful angels.

God is incredibly patient with all humans, and he loves people as his finest creation. However, God will use his warrior angels to bring swift and extreme judgment against those who stubbornly oppose him and willfully seek to endanger his children. God does not make war against his creation without necessity. His strong reaction to evil is a necessary response against those who seek to overthrow him as Lord. God uses angels to protect his creation, to defeat his enemy, and to advance his progress toward eternity.

Points to Remember

- God does not take the matter of warring against people lightly. However, when necessary, he will use angels to fight in these conflicts, bringing heavy losses to humans.

  - Angels have also warred against their rebellious fellow angels. There are two faithful angels for every rebellious demon.

Check Your Understanding

- **Why is it important to understand the power of angels?**

It is important to understand that angels are powerful beings created by God to do what he commands. This includes making war against all his enemies, whether they are angelic or human.

- **What is significant about the angelic actions against humans recorded in the Bible?**

It is significant to understand that angels act against God's enemies only at God's command. They do not act against humans who follow God by faith, and they do not oppose humans the way Satan opposes humans.

The Role of Fallen Angels in Temptation, Possession, and Sin

People throughout time have been mesmerized by the possibility of human interaction with spirit beings. Angels and demons hover figuratively in the collective imagination of the population and literally as they engage in human affairs throughout time. Because of this, fact and fantasy have often been confused. Just what is the role of these beings in tempting people to disobey God? Demonic possession is both fascinating and frightening. A biblical understanding of these important subjects can serve both as warning and as reassurance.

✼

In the Gospel accounts of the ministry of Jesus, the Bible introduces people who were troubled beyond the limits of human understanding. These people are described as being possessed by demons. The manner in which these people behaved frightened others in their community and caused the people themselves either to seek Jesus for help or to isolate themselves from human interaction. While the possessed people terrified others, Jesus never demonstrated fear in healing them from their spiritual oppression.

It's in Christ that you . . . found yourselves home free—signed, sealed, and delivered by the Holy Spirit.

Ephesians 1:13 MSG

The demons had gone out of him, and he was sitting there at the feet of Jesus. He had clothes on and was in his right mind.

Luke 8:35 CEV

One such man who was wrought with demons is known in the Bible as "the Gadarene demoniac." As a man who was controlled by the evil spirits of demons, he was known in the Gadarene region as the man who lived in the cemetery in the outskirts of the community. He had been bound in chains but had broken free. He was known for tearing at his own flesh, speaking in a nonhuman voice, and running naked through the land. He invoked fear in everyone who lived in the area. Even so, Jesus approached the man without fear or apprehension. Jesus spoke directly to the multitude of demons that enslaved the man. The demons acknowledged that Jesus is God, and begged him not to condemn them to the fiery pit. They were powerless against Jesus, and they submitted without resistance when he cast them into a nearby herd of pigs. Once Jesus liberated the man from the demons, the man sat quietly at the foot of Jesus in total control and with peace of mind.

Jesus freed many others from demonic possession while he ministered on the earth. The Bible reports that he drove away several oppressive spirits from Mary Magdalene. He healed demon-possessed men who had been rendered blind or mute by their oppressors. The Bible says that all those who were possessed by demons were cured when Jesus spoke to them. No evidence exists of any demon who could withstand the commands of Jesus to flee from the humans they possessed.

Ironically, Jesus himself was accused of performing his miracles by the power of a demon that possessed him. Jesus refuted this false allegation, and in so doing revealed important truth. He declared that it was impossible for a demon to dwell in a place that belonged to God. Specifically, no demon would be able to overpower and control any person who belongs to God by faith in Jesus Christ. The Bible promises that when God saves a person from hell and promises him or her heaven, the presence of the Holy Spirit is one evidence of this guarantee. The Bible declares that such a person has been "filled by the Spirit of God." This indwelling or "filling" is pictured as an overflowing manifestation of the presence of God in the person's life. This means that the person cannot and will not be possessed by Satan or a demon.

Even so, Christians are still subject to the temptation and deception of fallen angels. God permits and even ordains these occasional temptations as tests that are intended to prove people's faithfulness to God. The Bible promises that people will never be tempted beyond what they can withstand. God will always provide a way for people to escape any temptation. While Satan engages in temptation to deceive people, defy God, and destroy lives, God orchestrates testing in people's lives to bring spiritual victories, prove faith, and affirm God's promises.

> The unclean spirits, whenever they saw Him, fell down before Him and cried out, saying, "You are the Son of God."
>
> Mark 3:11 NKJV

It is important for every person to understand and appreciate the reality of fallen angels intermingling in the spiritual realm. These evil beings have the capability to bring spiritual, emotional, and mental misery to people who are alienated from God because of ignorance or disbelief. However, Jesus' power is available through the Holy Spirit to overcome any dark spiritual presence in the world today.

Myth Buster

Demon possession appears to be behind one of the significant misunderstandings of an important biblical personality. Historically, Mary Magdalene has been described as a woman who had formerly been a prostitute before deciding to follow Jesus. However, there is no biblical evidence that Mary was ever engaged in such a scandalous profession. Rather, Mary is described as  having been freed by Jesus from the possession of seven demons. Many scholars reason that it was demon possession that led people to label Mary as a prostitute, even though she likely was not. Regardless, she was freed from her past by faith in Jesus.

Points to Remember

- Demon possession in the Bible was a real and supernatural phenomenon. It caused people to behave in unnatural, dangerous ways that frightened others and caused the people to become alienated from everyone else.

- Jesus demonstrated the consistent ability to free people from demon possession. No demon could withstand the command of Jesus to flee from a person and cease oppressing them. Every spirit submitted to the orders of Jesus.

- Jesus promised that any person today whose faith is in God would be protected from demon possession and spiritual oppression by the filling and fulfilling presence of the Holy Spirit in the person's life.

- God's presence in a person's life brings sanity, mental clarity, peace of mind, and a calm demeanor.

Check Your Understanding

- **If it is impossible for a demon to possess a Christian, what will God permit in demon interaction with Christians, and why?**

God permits Christians to be tested by demons so that his children may resist the temptations of Satan and prove their faith in God as an example to others, that they may be encouraged and grow in their own faith.

- **How does a person "test the spirits" to determine if the spirit is a messenger of God or an agent of Satan?**

Any person can evaluate the message of a spirit being by comparing its message to what God has already revealed in the Bible. If the spirit's message agrees with biblical truth, it can be trusted. If the message does not agree with biblical truth, it cannot be trusted.

FAQ—What Is the Role of Angels in a Person's Death?

It is nearly incomprehensible that a person can be fully alive in the physical world one minute and then the next minute be ushered into the fullness of the spiritual world. This is hard to understand because we humans are experientially bound to our bodies. To imagine a real, complete existence without the body is virtually inconceivable. Nonetheless, the Bible teaches that each person passes instantly from the physical life to the spiritual life. To accomplish this feat, God uses angels, his heavenly messengers.

✳

The Bible's book of Luke records an account given by Jesus where a poor man named Lazarus and a wealthy man both died. Lazarus passed instantly from the physical life into the spiritual realm with God, and the wealthy man instantly found himself separated from God by a great, impassable chasm.

Jesus included details about how we go from the physical life to the spiritual life. Jesus said, "The time came when the beggar died and the angels carried him to Abraham's side" (Luke 16:22 NIV). The crowd listening to Jesus understood that his reference to Abraham meant Lazarus immediately went to heaven and angels delivered him there.

By Him all things were created that are in heaven and that are on earth, visible and invisible. . . . All things were created through Him and for Him.

Colossians 1:16 NKJV

The harvest is the end of the age; and the reapers are angels.

Matthew 13:39 NASB

God created angels, who are spirit beings, to perform multitudes of tasks and do his bidding in all matters. One such task given to angels is to usher us from the physical life into the spiritual life. Jesus taught that angels are responsible for separating the souls who would be in heaven from those who would be in hell. He warned listeners, "The angels will come and separate the wicked from the righteous" (Matthew 13:49 NIV). Jesus' story about Lazarus explained that the poor man was carried to heaven by angels. The rich man was described as being "in hell and in torment" (Luke 16:23 MSG). While some effort has been made to interpret this story as a parable, Jesus was revealing the truth about how angels deliver souls to their eternal destinations.

Points to Remember

• After physical death, everyone will immediately find himself either in heaven or in hell. There is no exchange between these two realms.

• Though the details are not explicit as to how people are carried to heaven or delivered to hell, biblical teaching is clear that angels are responsible for transporting people to their eternal destination.

Check Your Understanding

▪ **What are angels, and what is their task in relation to the death of a person?**

Angels are nonhuman beings created by God to do his bidding. One task God has assigned to them is transporting people after physical death to heaven or to hell.

▪ **Why is it important to understand that angels have the responsibility of transporting people to their eternal destination?**

It is important to understand that angels do this in obedience to God, whose bidding is the final authority.

FAQ—How Do You Relate to Angelic Beings in This Life?

Several times in the Bible, God determined to use angels to communicate with humans. These interactions are presented with consistent clarity, and they offer important insight into how angels interact with humans. The modern world is one where the fallen angel Satan continues to deceive as many people as possible. At the same time, much of the world seeks spiritual insight and understanding. Reports of angelic visitations are numerous. Comparing these reports to examples in the Bible allows people today to determine the experience's authenticity, and to know whether the visitation was from a friend or foe.

In the numerous biblical accounts of people being visited by angels, there are some common elements in the encounters, elements that reveal the natural reaction to such otherworldly visitations. The angels are consistently described as shining with a brightness of God's holiness. Repeatedly, this manifestation of the purity of God caused an immediate response from the people who witnessed it:

Satan himself is disguised as an angel of light.

2 Corinthians 11:14 HCSB

The LORD spoke kind and comforting words to the angel who talked with me. Then the angel who was speaking to me said, "Proclaim this word: This is what the LORD Almighty says."

Zechariah 1:13–14 NIV

- Abraham bowed before the angels who would later destroy Sodom and Gomorrah.

- Lot bowed his face to the ground in their presence.

- The pagan false prophet Balaam fell to his face when he saw the Lord's angel.

- The true prophet Isaiah was completely undone from a vision of God and the heavenly host of angels.

- The prophet Daniel fell on his face in the presence of God's angel.

- In the New Testament, Zechariah, John the Baptist's father, was seized with fear when he was met by Gabriel.

- Even though Gabriel's message to Mary was a wonderful blessing, she was troubled by his visit.

- The shepherds were greatly frightened by the angels who announced the birth of Jesus to Mary and Joseph.

- The apostle John fell on his face in the presence of an angel while given his vision of the future as recorded in Revelation.

Whenever it was important for an angel to demonstrate that he was sent by God, he showed God's holy nature in his appearance. Accordingly, the natural response of the human was to fall forward or bow to God as represented by the angel.

When an angel appeared before a person, it was always for a purpose. Typically, it was to communicate an important message. Accordingly, it was important for the person to understand the message and be able to respond to it. Unfortunately, the first example of human-angelic interaction was the exchange between Adam and Eve and Satan. To the first people, the fallen angel appeared as a serpent and deceived them to doubt God's goodness, to distrust his plan, and to disobey his instructions. Adam and Eve did not test the claims of Satan against what they already knew about God. Instead, they compared the accusations of Satan against their own emotions, desires, and assumptions. The tragic result of their errors was the breakdown of their perfect relationship with God.

In subsequent examples of communication between angels and humans, however, the situations demonstrate that everything that is communicated by an angel of God to a person will always be in agreement with what God has already promised or revealed. Angelic messages of judgment, of victory, or of blessing were in agreement with earlier God-given promises. In this, God used angels to prove his faithfulness or to demonstrate his commitment to complete what he started with a promise given much earlier in history.

The principles established in these biblical examples can serve as a method to "test the spirits" while living in the physical life. Until eternity in heaven arrives, any encounter with angels must be subject to examination and evaluation. The Bible says that Satan presents himself as an angel of light; it is impossible to make a determination of the goodness or intent of an angel based upon what the human sees in the encounter. Anything revealed by an angel of God will be in agreement with truth that has already been established by God through the Bible. If an angelic being attempts to convince a person that God is not good or that God cannot be trusted, or if an angelic being attempts to lead the person to disobey God, that person can be certain that the being is a fallen angel. While authentic visits by angels are rare and provocative, everyone can have confidence to assess the experience to determine whether the angel is of God or of Satan.

> The angel said, "Don't be afraid. I'm here to announce a great and joyful event that is meant for everybody, worldwide."
>
> Luke 2:10 MSG

Myth Buster

Good angels are popularly depicted as human babies. Evil angels or demons are depicted as red devils with pitchforks. In numerous encounters with humans, angels appear to take on the form of a person. In the visions of heaven, angels appear to have wings but are otherwise nonhuman in appearance. Some angels  appear to have faces that resemble animal faces but with unexplainable features such as eyes covering all parts of their bodies. While some people interpret these biblical descriptions as literal depictions of angels, others interpret these descriptions as symbolic of the nature or abilities of angels.

Points to Remember

• As messengers of God, angels have at rare times inter-acted with humans to communicate a message from God. In these encounters, the humans usually fell forward in an act of worship to God.

• When an angel brings a message from God, that message can be tested against the Bible for its validity. God has declared that he will not speak a message through an angel that contradicts what he has already revealed in the Bible.

• People should not evaluate an angelic message based upon their own emotions, desires, or preconceived notions, as the cautionary example of Adam and Eve demonstrates. Satan will attempt to deceive people by getting them to doubt God, distrust him, and disobey him.

Check Your Understanding

▪ **What is the significance of the fact that Balaam and Lot responded to their angelic visitors in the same way as did Daniel and Abraham?**

The fact that all four of these men responded to God's angels by bowing demonstrates that in the presence of God's holiness, all humans will worship the Lord.

▪ **What does Adam and Eve's encounter with Satan demonstrate to people about Satan's tactics in interacting with humans?**

Satan demonstrated that he would appear in a way that is agreeable to humans. He will then connive to deceive humans to disobey God and doubt his love for them.

▪ **What does it mean to "test the spirits"?**

"Testing the spirits" means to use the Bible to evaluate the validity and trustworthiness of a message communicated by an angelic being.

FAQ—How Will You Relate to Angels in Eternity?

The interaction between humans and angels throughout history has been intense, even when in the majority of circumstances the encounters were not adversarial. Humans typically have responded in fear or ignorance when relating to angels. However, the future offers a different plan for how God's messengers will interact with God's children. The heavenly relationship between humans and angels promises to be cooperative and harmonious. It is evident from the promises of the Bible that all beings will experience eternity in unity with one another.

The Bible offers encouraging glimpses of future relationship between angels and humans. In eternity, the angels will rejoice, singing songs of praise to Jesus because God's restoration of people will be complete. God's justice will have been perfectly executed. All the rebellious spirits—human and angelic—will be eternally separated from God forever. Every person who belongs in heaven will be in heaven. There will be no more temptation, no more failure, no more rebellion, no more disobedience, and no more warfare. There will be joyful, peace-filled coexistence with God's perfect angels, and humans will be restored to the perfection of their original design.

> It was revealed to them that they were not serving themselves but you. . . . Angels desire to look into these things.
>
> 1 Peter 1:12 HCSB
>
> Don't you realize that we will judge angels?
>
> 1 Corinthians 6:3 NLT

Because humans and angels will perfectly coexist, humans will join the angels in the song of rejoicing that praises God forever. This indicates that humans will be in a continual state of joy in heaven. The Bible gives provocative hints that even though angels are advantaged beyond humans now, they look forward to the inauguration of eternity when that relationship will change. In eternity, humans will have the authority to judge the angels. In heaven, the angels will look to humans to learn and understand the deep things of God that they themselves do not understand. This means not only that the lessons learned by faith in this life will be remembered forever but also that they will be a blessing that humans share with angels to teach them new understanding.

Points to Remember

• In heaven, humans and angels will rejoice together in unity over the fulfillment of God's work being accomplished now. The advantages held by angels over humans will change in eternity.

• The angels look forward to eternity because they do not understand all that they currently do in obedience. In heaven, they will learn important spiritual truth from the humans.

Check Your Understanding

▪ **What is the present relationship between humans and angels?**

In the present relationship between angels and humans, angels willingly do their current tasks with joy, even though they currently have advantages over humans.

▪ **What are ways the relationship between humans and angels will change in eternity?**

In heaven, the angels will understand from humans the way to relate to God that humans learned during the physical life. Also, humans will be given authority in heaven to judge the angels.

FAQ—Are Angels Really People with Wings?

The world is fascinated by angels. Popular television programs have been broadcast for years that feature angelic beings as the lead characters. Movies base dynamic plots on human/angelic interaction. Books, artwork, and music fuel an unceasing interest in the spiritual realm of angels. Unfortunately for people who really want to know about angels, much of what is presented as fact is nothing more than creative fantasy. Chief among the myths about angels is that they are celestial humans. In fact, the Bible reveals that in many important ways, angels and humans are completely different.

Angels and humans are both created beings. The Bible indicates, however, that all angels were created as eternal spiritual beings as part of the original creation. No additional angels were created after the initial creation. Humans, though, were created differently. The Bible reveals that God knew every person he would ever create prior to actually creating the heavens and the earth. However, humans have been created throughout history by the normal biological processes that God has ordained. Likewise, humans must die at the end of their physical lives. This is the consequence for rebellion against God. Each person's spirit and soul will continue for eternity in either heaven or hell. Angels, though, never die. The angels who oppose God as part of the satanic rebellion will one day be cast into the eternal lake of fire, and the angels who

Those who are counted worthy to attain that age, and the resurrection from the dead, neither marry nor are given in marriage; nor can they die anymore, for they are equal to the angels and are sons of God, being sons of the resurrection.

Luke 20:35 36 NKJV

You are all sons of God through faith in Christ Jesus.

Galatians 3:26 NASB

remained true will remain in heaven forever under the authority of Jesus and humans.

While the two named angels of the Lord, Gabriel and Michael, have masculine names and are understood in masculine terms, angels themselves are spirit beings that are neither male nor female. They were created as a fixed quantity of beings, and their population does not increase through angelic procreation. Conversely, humans started from the union of Adam and Eve. Throughout the generations, and despite natural disasters and supernatural judgment, the number of humans has increased.

In the Bible, Jesus is the Son of God, but angels are described as the "sons of God." This term can be confusing, and it seemingly contradicts the notion that angels are neither male nor female. In some references where this term is used, it speaks specifically to fallen angels who mated with human women. This provocative account could mean either that

these demonic beings took a male form, somewhat in the manner that the obedient angels Michael and Gabriel appeared as males, or that the demons actually possessed human males. Beyond these limited references, the term *sons of God* used to reference angels actually speaks to the relationship of angels to God, not to the angels' sex. Angels relate to God as children. He is the heavenly Father who created them. This is the same distinction given to humans who, by their faith, belong to God as his children.

Angels have their home in heaven and their specific assignments on earth. They are limited in this regard, but they interact between the physical and spiritual realms in a way that exceeds human ability. While angels are able to do only what they have been assigned to do or given permission to accomplish upon the earth, they are able to traverse the two realms as necessary. Humans, however, have no ability to physically interact with the spiritual realm apart from faith efforts such as prayer. Only after death to the physical life will humans experience the spiritual realm where God and angels freely and fully exist.

Ironically, most of these differences are highlighted in the Bible's promise that one day humans will be like angels. This means that in heaven, humans will behave like angels by being in total unity with God, and they will have some characteristics that are common to angels. The Bible says that whether a person is male or female on earth is immaterial in heaven. People's marital relationships on earth will pale in heaven in comparison to people's perfect union with Jesus in heaven.

Only those people who are led by God's Spirit are his children.

Romans 8:14 CEV

Despite having these traits in common with angels, humans in heaven will remain distinct from angels. Humans never have been angels, nor will humans ever become angels. Angels exist to serve God. In heaven, angels will be subject to humans. People will exercise a God-given ability to judge angels and exercise humble authority over these unique spiritual beings.

Myth Buster

A popular myth suggests that children who die as infants or toddlers become cherub angels. This false notion has been popularized primarily through ancient artwork dating back to the fifteenth century that depicted cherubic angels as pudgy, rosy-cheeked, tiny-winged infants hovering above humans. Cupid, the mythical "god of love," is often presented as a cherubic angel, sometimes 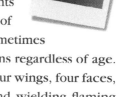 even wearing a diaper. In reality, humans are humans regardless of age. Angelic cherubs are described biblically as having four wings, four faces, being covered with eyes, having human hands, and wielding flaming swords.

Points to Remember

• Angels are created beings who are neither male nor female. They were created all together at the dawn of creation.

• Humans were created male and female. In heaven, whether a person is male or female is immaterial.

• Both angels and humans are described biblically as "sons of God." This term does not refer to the identity of angels as male, nor that humans and angels are the same nature. However, it does refer to the reality that both angels and humans have been created by God and can relate to him in a personal way.

Check Your Understanding

▪ **How are angels and humans different?**

Angels and humans were created different. They are different in their nature and their purpose. They are different in how they relate to one another and how they relate to God. Angels exist differently within the physical and spiritual realm of creation than do humans.

▪ **How are angels and humans similar?**

Both angels and humans were created to relate with God in a personal way. Obedient angels and humans who accept God's offer of heaven will spend eternity in heaven with God.

▪ **Why is it important to understand how angels and humans are different?**

It is important to understand how angels differ from humans because of the extensive confusion regarding the nature and reality of angels. It is also important because angels and humans will have real relationships with one another in heaven for eternity.

FAQ—When Did God Create Angels?

In the Bible's creation account, there is no specific information regarding the creation of angels. Every other aspect of creation is mentioned, yet information about when God made his heavenly messengers is not revealed. Later books of prophecy introduce the existence of angels and show some of the important responsibilities that angels undertake in obedience to the command of God. Lucifer is revealed as a fallen angel who led an angelic rebellion. Reading through the Scriptures, it become apparent that angels were an early step in God's creative process.

In the first two chapters of Genesis, the creation account is told both in detail and in summary. Over six days, God created the heavens and the earth, the waters and the skies, the sun and the moon and the stars, the waters of the earth and the high ground, the plants and the animals, and ultimately the humans. God reflected on all that he had created and declared it to be good. Nowhere in either of these accounts is there mention of the creation of angels.

The third chapter of Genesis opens with the introduction of "the serpent," the snakelike embodiment of the personality named Satan. In

Where were you when I created the earth? Tell me, since you know so much! Who decided on its size? Certainly you'll know that! Who came up with the blueprints and measurements? How was its foundation poured, and who set the cornerstone, while the morning stars sang in chorus and all the angels shouted praise? And who took charge of the ocean when it gushed forth like a baby from the womb? That was me!

Job 38:4–9 MSG

the books of Isaiah and Ezekiel, the Bible reveals that *Satan* ("adversary") is the title given to the angel Lucifer, the angel who was responsible for protecting the glory of God but who was cast out from heaven because of his pride and jealousy against God. Considering these details alone, it is unclear when God created angels.

It is evident, however, that it is important to discern when angels were created. For example, if angels were created after the creation of humans, this creation occurred after God had labeled his creation "good" and after God's self-appointed time of rest. The implication of this is that angels were not created "good" and that God's work of creation was not complete. This would mean that no angel could be trusted and that the entire premise of the "day of rest" would be invalid.

However, Genesis 2:1 reveals that everything in the heavens and the earth had been completed by the end of the sixth day. This would 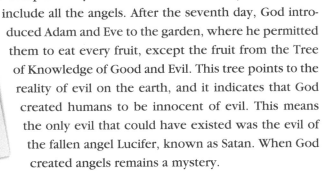 include all the angels. After the seventh day, God introduced Adam and Eve to the garden, where he permitted them to eat every fruit, except the fruit from the Tree of Knowledge of Good and Evil. This tree points to the reality of evil on the earth, and it indicates that God created humans to be innocent of evil. This means the only evil that could have existed was the evil of the fallen angel Lucifer, known as Satan. When God created angels remains a mystery.

A possible insight into this mystery is revealed in a third chronological account of the creation: "By the word of the LORD the heavens were made, and all the host of them by the breath of His mouth. He gathers the waters of the sea together as a heap; He lays up the deep in storehouses" (Psalm 33:6–7 NKJV). By comparing this account with the accounts in Genesis 1 and 2, it can be seen that all three accounts agree that God creates by the power of his spoken will. All three accounts agree that God first created the heavens, and that he followed this up by creating the waters of the sea. However, Psalm 33 provocatively includes the detail that the "host of them" (the heavens) was created after the creation of the heavens and before the creation of the seas. This would mean that the angels were created between Genesis 1:1 and Genesis 1:2.

The validity of this possibility will likely not be known until history concludes. However, this consideration offers implications that agree with what is known and established in accepted biblical doctrine: Angels were an essential part of early creation, Lucifer and a third of the

> God created everything in the heavenly realms and on earth. He made the things we can see and the things we can't see.
>
> Colossians 1:16 NLT

angels fell prior to the creation of man, and God's plan was set and established before he declared it "good." This scenario provides for supportable doctrines regarding the messenger servants of God, as well as for the fallen angels that are today known as demons. Finally, this possibility helps explain why the fallen angels fervently oppose both God and humans, and it justifies their eternal condemnation at the close of human history.

Myth Buster

With much confusion existing about angels, a common misperception of angels is related to the nature of their being. Many people mistakenly believe that angels are the heavenly souls of humans, that the natural evolution of a person who dies is to go to heaven and become an angel. However, the Bible clearly teaches that angels and humans are distinctly different and share only the fact that both are created beings. Angels were created chronologically before humans, but humans were created to be above the angels.

Points to Remember

• The creation of angels is not mentioned in either of the first two chapters of Genesis, where the account of God's creation is both told and retold.

- The psalmist revealed that angels were created after God created the heavens but before he created the waters of the deep.

- By making the angels early in the universal creation process and providing a comprehensive plan to account for Satan's deception of Adam and Eve, God was able to review the totality of creation and label it all as "good."

Check Your Understanding

- **Why does it matter that Satan is introduced in Genesis 3, even though there is no account of the creation of the angels prior to this reference?**

This is significant because it reveals that the angels had been created by this time and because Lucifer and the angels had already rebelled against God and had been cast from heaven.

- **What is the significance of God labeling his creation "good" if the angelic creation and rebellion had already occurred by this time?**

This is significant because it demonstrates that God created the earth and humans with a purpose. He created people with the intent to restore them, knowing they would succumb to Satan's evil.

- **Why is it important that the angels were created after the heavens but before the waters?**

It is important that the angels were created after the heavens because it shows that God created them to exist in the highest heaven with him. Their creation prior to the waters shows that God had a place to expel those who rebelled against him.

FAQ—What Are the Limitations of Angels?

Angels have strength that far exceeds human ability. When compared to human transportation, the travel of angels appears virtually unrestricted. Angels demonstrate wisdom and insight that allow them to comprehend God's plan in ways that humans can only meagerly apprehend by faith. However, God has limited angels in important ways. The restrictions placed upon angels always point to the power of God in directing time's march toward eternity. Restrictions also point to his commitment to use every resource he created to accomplish his divine purpose.

Because of the angels' abilities, it is tempting to view angels as superhuman or semidivine. However, angels are altogether nonhuman. Humans who die do not become angels, and angels never have been nor will they ever be human. The only thing that angels and humans have in common is that they are both types of beings created by God. Accordingly, both are limited in their abilities. According to the Bible, humans have been created with lesser abilities than the angels have. However, God holds humans in a higher regard than he holds angels. In eternity, humans will have authority over angels and angels will serve humans in perfect obedience to God.

What is man that You are mindful of him. . . . You have made him a little lower than the angels.

Hebrews 2:6–7 NKJV

Heaven and earth will pass away. . . . But of that day or hour no one knows, not even the angels in heaven, nor the Son, but the Father alone.

Mark 13:31–32 NASB

Angels express significant advantages in power, stamina, wisdom, and physical abilities in the temporary reality of earthly life. Perhaps this is because angels—both obedient and rebellious—exist with ease equally between the physical and spiritual realities, whereas the human experience with the spiritual reality is understood primarily by faith until after death occurs. Obedient angels are able to make sudden appearances in the audience of humans, and they typically reflect the glory of God in a way that is overwhelming and frightening to the humans they encounter. Angels are powerful, but not all-powerful. They are present when unseen, but they are not omnipresent. They are wise, but not omniscient. Obedient angels love humans as God's finest creation and look forward to eternity where their service to God is fully rendered in deference to the humans in heaven.

Points to Remember

• Angels demonstrate incredible feats of strength and insight into God's plans that far surpass human limitations. However, angels are not all-powerful and all-knowing. God has limited their abilities.

• In heaven, angels and humans will have a more equitable relationship. Humans will have bodies that have been perfected, and all God's creatures will live fully in the eternal spiritual reality.

Check Your Understanding

▪ **Why are angels more powerful than humans?**

Angels have more power than humans in the current physical reality because they live in complete unity with God. They exist with equal comfort between the physical realm and the spiritual realm in ways that humans will not experience until after they go to the eternal heaven.

▪ **How will the relationship between angels and humans change in heaven?**

In the physical reality, humans have been created lower than angels. In heaven, humans will have authority and responsibility over angels.

Satan in the Afterlife

Satan is the author of confusion. God wants every person to escape confusion about the evil ways, dark tactics, and certain future of the fallen angel who hates people and dares to oppose God.

Contents

The Origin of Satan 167

The Ambition of Satan..171

The Animosity of Satan..173

The Tactics of Satan 175

The Partners of Satan 177

The Defeat of Satan 181

The Punishment of Satan...185

FAQ—Is Satan Really Real?..187

FAQ—What Are Satan's Limitations?..189

We don't want to unwittingly give Satan an opening for yet more mischief—we're not oblivious to his sly ways!

2 Corinthians 2:11 MSG

The Origin of Satan

The Bible tells of a glorious angel of the highest rank who dwelt on the mountain of God in heaven. He was wonderfully made and perfectly created. However, this beautiful creature became jealous of God and built up pride in his heart. He set his mind to be like God. With a legion of accomplices, he rebelled. His foolish effort was swiftly crushed. Cast to the earth, he and his cohorts bide the time before their final judgment, deceiving humans and destroying lives in spiteful acts of rebellion against God.

There was a time at the dawn of creation when Lucifer, that prideful angel, was an angel of honor. His name meant "shining one." He was a cherub, the rank of angels responsible for defending the holiness of God. Lucifer was perfectly made and served God with unmatched wisdom. The Bible describes him in terms of majesty and brilliance and compares his appearance to flawless gems radiating the glory of God. Isaiah 14:12 describes him as "O shining star, son of the morning!" (NLT). Some religious scholars believe that Lucifer had angelic authority over the universe and the earth and was responsible for protecting God's glory among his creation.

You were blameless in your ways from the day you were created until unrighteousness was found in you.

Ezekiel 28:15 NASB

How you are fallen from heaven, O Lucifer, son of the morning! How you are cut down to the ground, you who weakened the nations!

Isaiah 14:12 NKJV

However, at some undetermined time early in God's process of creation, Lucifer stored pride within himself. He considered himself equal to the one who created him. He thought that he deserved the glory that was directed to God, and he decided that he was like God. Lucifer's defiance was not part of his nature; rather, it was a spontaneous reaction that sprang from his jealousy of God.

Lucifer's insurgence was not merely a revolutionary attitude or belligerent mind-set. He was actually filled with violence against God and God's creation. As a cherub, Lucifer's following included one-third of all the angels, and those angels joined him in rebellion against God.

Lucifer and his league of rebel angels established themselves in opposition to God. This required God to address the situation swiftly in accord with his holy nature. God declared Lucifer guilty of a multitude of offenses and issued an immediate judgment against him and his cohorts. He expelled them all from heaven, casting them into the universe and particularly to the earth.

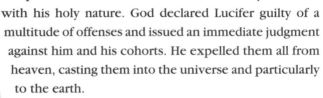

Banished from heaven, their animosity against God increased. Lucifer was then known by the title *Satan*, which means "adversary." As the adversary who opposes God, he plots his rebellion and connives with the fallen angels, identified then as demons. His pride rotted him, and the glory that once reflected the holiness of God was replaced by the muck of his degradation. Satan wishes for a future where God is defeated, he is vindicated, and he is worshiped as God.

Humans have become a special object of Satan's wrath. He knows that humans are God's finest creation and the specific object of God's love, even more so than angels are. Accordingly, Satan hates all humans with unmatched hostility. This loathing manifested itself in his deception of Adam and Eve, which damaged the relationship between God and his people. Satan, challenged by God's declaration that Job was the finest man on earth, afflicted Job and attacked everything that fine man held dear. Satan continues his efforts against people today. He is everywhere people are. He is devoted to destroying as many lives as possible in his continuing hostility toward God.

Satan is unable to keep God from accomplishing his plan. God's plan will prevail. In the days of Jesus, the demons demonstrated their awareness of the certainty of their future. Satan alone, in an attempt to reign over him, was audacious enough to tempt Jesus. He fled in fear when he realized that he had no hope of victory in that futile effort. Jesus encountered multiple demons who were tormenting people in acts of evil and violence against God. When confronted by Jesus, the demons consistently acknowledged him as Lord, thinking the promised time of their eternal judgment in the lake of fire had arrived. Satan and his demons know their future, and the clock of history continues to progress toward the day of their unavoidable defeat at the hands of Jesus Christ.

> There was a great fiery red dragon. . . . His tail swept away a third of the stars in heaven and hurled them to the earth.
>
> Revelation 12:3–4 HCSB

Myth Buster

Legends refer to Lucifer as the worship leader of heaven prior to his fall as Satan. These legends originate in the translation of biblical passages describing the angel Lucifer. In detailing the appearance of the cherub, the book of Ezekiel describes him as being adorned by tambourines, timbrels, and pipes. However, no explicit references refer to Lucifer's leading the worship of God in heaven. Instead, the mention of these instruments identified with Lucifer indicates that worshiping God is an essential part of the angels' identity, particularly that of the cherub who was responsible for defending God's holiness.

Points to Remember

• Lucifer was a cherub, perfectly created as an angel who walked in the presence of God and was given authority by God.

• Lucifer rebelled against God because he selfishly desired the glory and praise that God rightfully received.

• Lucifer and one-third of the angels who followed him were cast to the earth for rebelling against God. Lucifer is now known as *Satan,* the "adversary."

Check Your Understanding

▪ **Why is it important to understand that Lucifer was perfectly made?**

It is important to understand that Lucifer was perfectly made because it demonstrates that he is responsible for the evil that resulted in his expulsion from heaven.

▪ **What does it mean that he was a cherub?**

The rank of cherub is that of a high-ranking angel given important responsibilities in heaven. Lucifer was given immense authority and privilege in heaven, and was assigned to protect God's glory. Instead, Lucifer became jealous of it and attempted to steal it.

▪ **Why does it matter that one-third of all the angels joined Lucifer in his rebellion against God?**

The fact that one-third of all angels rebelled against God reveals that Lucifer was not alone in his rebellion. This is important in understanding how Satan is at work in the world today.

The Ambition of Satan

Lucifer enjoyed the high honor of protecting the glory of God. He called Eden, the garden of God, his home. He walked in God's presence and served as God's guardian. He was adorned beautifully. Yet the unmatched honor he experienced was inadequate to satisfy his desires. His lust to be like God led him to oppose his Creator. Even now, thousands of years later, Satan pursues the overthrow of God, and he still wants to rule over creation, despite his knowledge of his eventual defeat and imprisonment in the lake of fire.

Even after Satan was expelled from heaven, he determined to make the earth and the universe the domain of his rule. The Bible calls him the "ruler of the kingdom of the air" and the "spirit who is now at work in those who are now disobedient" (Ephesians 2:2 NIV). Although Satan is unable to create anything on his own in the manner that God created everything by spoken word, Satan's pride blinded him, and he seeks to rule over a creation that he had no part in making.

Satan is recognized as having authority over the earth during this time of history when humanity is separated from God because of human disobedience. In this regard, Satan's efforts are seen in proliferating strife, disease, and evil throughout the world. The fact that the church exists, thrives, and succeeds in this fallen, conflicted world is evidence that God loves people and has not given them up to Satan.

In much buying and selling you turned violent, you sinned! I threw you, disgraced, off the mountain of God.

Ezekiel 28:16 MSG

Anyone who keeps on sinning belongs to the devil. He has sinned from the beginning, but the Son of God came to destroy all that he has done.

1 John 3:8 CEV

Satan's defeat is certain and his imprisonment will be eternal. Satan knows that this will happen, but he does not know when, so he continues with his maddened rampage. He continues to lie, deceive, and destroy as many people as possible. In this dangerous environment, however, God's Holy Spirit is alive and active, and he daily leads people to believe in Jesus' message of hope for eternal life.

Points to Remember

- Lucifer was blessed with great authority as a cherub in Eden.

- Satan has authority on the earth and in the universe as a fallen angel living in a "fallen" creation.

- Satan's authority will end, and he will experience hell as a prisoner.

Check Your Understanding

- **What is Satan's ambition?**

Satan's ambition is to be worshiped as God. He desires to rule over God's creation, sitting in God's throne as Lord.

- **Why is it important to understand that Satan's earthly authority is temporary?**

It is important to understand that Satan's authority is temporary in order to have a proper understanding that he, too, will face God's judgment and punishment for his rebellion.

The Animosity of Satan

The world's misunderstanding of Satan has created an incorrect perception of how he relates to humans. Some people foolishly worship him; others simply ignore him or think of him as an imaginary creation like Santa Claus or the Easter Bunny. Some people mistakenly trivialize him, and others worry excessively about him. Understanding how Satan relates to humans helps people keep an appropriate perspective.

Satan hates all people equally. He doesn't hate ungodly or evil people any more than he hates godly people. He doesn't hate atheists any more than he hates Christians. He doesn't hate murderers any more than he hates monks. He hates all people equally because every human is a creation of God, and Satan hates God. Humans were created in God's image, so every time Satan sees humans, he sees the handiwork of God, and Satan is filled with blind, prideful rage. Accordingly, Satan has committed his earthbound existence to lies, accusations, and deceptions. Satan will do everything in his ability to utterly destroy them.

The thief comes only to steal and kill and destroy; I have come that they may have life, and have it to the full.

John 10:10 NIV

You belong to God, my dear children. You have already won a victory over those people, because the Spirit who lives in you is greater than the spirit who lives in the world.

1 John 4:4 NLT

People are wise to be alert to Satan's efforts to attack people. Satan's driving ambition is to lead people to death and destruction. Satan uses every worldly weapon to accomplish this aim: addictions, laziness, success, and even other people. Those who are aware of Satan's ploys can overcome them. Faith, prayer, salvation, the Bible, and God's truth are just some of the tools God gives freely to his children to overcome the evil tactics of Satan. God desires all people to have victory over Satan, and he does not desire for anyone to be punished alongside Satan.

Points to Remember

- Satan hates all people. He wants everyone to be separated from God and alienated from God's love.

- Satan works tirelessly on the earth to bring accusations against people to God, to deceive people, and to destroy their lives.

Check Your Understanding

- **What does it mean to have a proper understanding of Satan?**

Having a proper understanding of Satan means understanding that Satan views humans with disgust and hatred.

- **Why is it important to know that Satan hates all people?**

It is important to understand that Satan hates all people so that nobody thinks he can please him or gain his favor by disobedience against God.

The Tactics of Satan

In the garden of Eden, Satan masterfully wove a tapestry of lies to deceive Adam and Eve. He convinced them that God could not be trusted, that they should question his goodness. They believed Satan's lies, and the consequences of their deception were enormous. From that time forward, all people were separated from an ongoing relationship with God in the physical life. Even now, thousands of years later, Satan employs the same tactics.

Satan's relentless agenda against humans is actually an attack against God. His strategy is remarkably consistent, even when it is creatively employed. In the earthly Paradise, God told Adam and Eve they could eat the fruit from any tree except the Tree of Knowledge of Good and Evil, for if they did, they would die. Satan confronted them, however, and led Eve to remember incorrectly what God had warned. Satan used her error to lie to them and say the reason God did not want them to eat the fruit of the Tree of Knowledge of Good and Evil was because if they did they would be like God. Wanting to believe Satan, Adam and Eve ate the fruit.

I have told you this, so that you might have peace in your hearts because of me. While you are in the world, you will have to suffer. But cheer up! I have defeated the world.

John 16:33 CEV

When the Liar speaks, he makes it up out of his lying nature and fills the world with lies.

John 8:44 MSG

Satan's tactic to separate people from a relationship with God follows the same pattern today. Everything a person needs to know to have a relationship with God has been revealed. However, the Enemy uses all the resources at his disposal to get people to doubt or forget what God has revealed to be true.

Thankfully, God foresaw Satan's scheme before creation, and God provided the remedy to the predicament. Everyone who trusts in God can overcome the tactics of Satan and be restored to a right relationship with God.

Points to Remember

- Satan's tactics do not change, even if they seem unique. He first deceives people into doubting God, and then he leads people to disobey God.

- God knew Satan's plan beforehand and provided the remedy to overcome it.

- Satan's attack against people is ultimately an attack against God himself.

Check Your Understanding

- **Why is it important to understand Satan's tactics?**

It is important to understand Satan's tactics because it helps people recognize when they are being led to doubt or disbelieve the promises of God, and they can avoid the consequences of being deceived by Satan.

- **What does it mean that Satan's attacks against people are ultimately an attack against God?**

Satan hates God, and Satan hates people as God's creation. When he successfully deceives people, he does so in an effort to oppose God. To Satan, humans are merely a casualty of his war against God.

The Partners of Satan

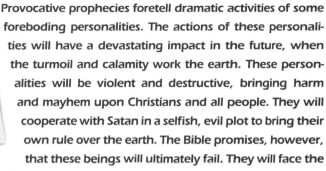

Provocative prophecies foretell dramatic activities of some foreboding personalities. The actions of these personalities will have a devastating impact in the future, when the turmoil and calamity work the earth. These personalities will be violent and destructive, bringing harm and mayhem upon Christians and all people. They will cooperate with Satan in a selfish, evil plot to bring their own rule over the earth. The Bible promises, however, that these beings will ultimately fail. They will face the unmerciful judgment of God.

Throughout human history, people have watched for the arrival of the man promised in the Bible to be God's Messiah. This man would be the one whom God had appointed and anointed to save the world, and particularly the Jewish people. According to the biblical predictions, the Messiah would be a king who would deliver the Jewish people from oppression and rule the world. His reign would usher in unprecedented peace and prosperity.

> The beast was seized, and with him the false prophet. . . . These two were thrown alive into the lake of fire which burns with brimstone.
>
> Revelation 19:20 NASB

> Beloved, do not believe every spirit, but test the spirits, whether they are of God; because many false prophets have gone out into the world.
>
> 1 John 4:1 NKJV

Many times in every age, men have stepped forward and identified themselves as the Messiah. Many people have claimed to have miraculous powers, and some have even claimed to be God in the flesh. However, only Jesus met all the prophetic requirements to be the Messiah. Accordingly, the Bible labels as "Antichrist" the impostors who aspired to fulfill the role of Messiah. The Bible states that history has seen many Antichrists, and they should be avoided.

The Bible foretells a person who will be the most deceptive, evil Antichrist of all when the clock of human history begins to wind down. In the future, Israel will find itself under global oppression, facing the overwhelming doom of global assault by surrounding neighbors. In this climate, a man will step in heroically and broker a peace between Israel and her enemies. The man will become a powerful world leader because of his historic action. However, midway through this peace treaty, the leader will break the treaty, unleashing a series of global calamities that will throw the world into chaos. In this environment, the leader will present himself as the Messiah and demand to be worshiped as God. The Bible foretells that this man will perform apparent miracles, which will deceive many people into worshiping him.

Joining him will be another world leader who will unite many of the world's religions and deceive them into worshiping the Antichrist as God. This deceptive religious leader is known in the Bible as the False Prophet. The False Prophet will deny the gospel of the Bible and will point instead to the Antichrist as the hope for humanity. He will broker unity among world religions that have historically been at odds, and they will join under the banner of worship to the Antichrist.

As the Antichrist and the False Prophet advance their devious scheme, they will establish an authoritarian government and singular religion. They will demand that all people submit to this authority and worship in this false system. Those who do not will likely pay the penalty of death for their decisions. Those who worship the Antichrist will bear an identifying mark, and a separate seal will identify Christians who oppose the Antichrist.

The Antichrist and the False Prophet will work in union with Satan. In fact, the Bible says that the Antichrist will actually be possessed by and controlled by Satan as he rules the world with tyranny. The Antichrist will establish himself in the Jewish temple in Jerusalem and desecrate it by demanding to be worshiped in it.

In this bleak setting of religious deception, global oppression, world-wide calamity, and Christian persecution, Jesus will return to the earth and defeat Satan, the Antichrist, and the False Prophet. Upon their defeat, Jesus will establish his earthly kingdom and rule as the true Messiah. He will reign upon the earth more than one thousand years in a time that will be marked by global peace and prosperity. The promises of God will be fulfilled as promised, and Jesus will overcome the unholy enemies who oppose him.

> Who is the liar? It is the man who denies that Jesus is the Christ. Such a man is the antichrist—he denies the Father and the Son.
>
> 1 John 2:22 NIV

Digging Deeper

Throughout history, many people have been accused of being the Antichrist. Perhaps most famously, the Roman emperor Nero was thought to be the Antichrist for his inhumane treatment and relentless persecution against Christians. Roman Catholic popes have been mistakenly accused, as have several U.S. presidents. Some scholars think the Antichrist will be European, while others believe he will be Jewish. Many people believe the Antichrist is alive today and that the conditions are right for the actions that would elevate him into global prominence and power. If these speculations are accurate, the stage is set for the end times that immediately precede eternity.

Points to Remember

• The Antichrist is a person who becomes a powerful world leader. He will initially be a peaceful leader, but ultimately he will lead a violent attack against Christians and will eventually claim to be God in the flesh.

• The False Prophet is the title given to the person who will become the most prominent religious leader in the world. This person will support the Antichrist's claims of divinity and deceive many people to worship the Antichrist as God.

• The cohorts of Satan will be defeated. They will be imprisoned first in hell and then eternally in the lake of fire.

Check Your Understanding

▪ **What is the difference between past Antichrists and the future Antichrist?**

Past Antichrists claimed to be God's Messiah, but they failed to fulfill the promises recorded in the Bible. The future Antichrist will be a powerful world leader who demands to be worshiped as God.

▪ **What is the role of the False Prophet?**

The False Prophet will be a future religious leader who will bring unity to the remaining world religions to worship the Antichrist as God in the flesh.

▪ **What is important to know about the future of the Antichrist and the False Prophet?**

It is important to remember that while the Antichrist and False Prophet are daunting figures in future history, both will be defeated by Jesus and both will be imprisoned in hell forever.

The Defeat of Satan

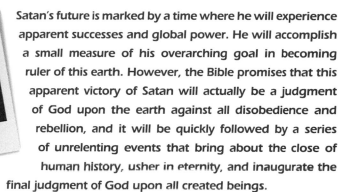

Satan's future is marked by a time where he will experience apparent successes and global power. He will accomplish a small measure of his overarching goal in becoming ruler of this earth. However, the Bible promises that this apparent victory of Satan will actually be a judgment of God upon the earth against all disobedience and rebellion, and it will be quickly followed by a series of unrelenting events that bring about the close of human history, usher in eternity, and inaugurate the final judgment of God upon all created beings.

✳

In the Bible's prophetic account of future events, Jesus will dramatically and gloriously appear upon the earth to claim victory over Satan, the Antichrist, and the False Prophet. When this happens, the Antichrist and the False Prophet will be cast into hell and Satan will be bound in chains and cast into the Abyss for one thousand years while Christ reigns upon the earth. During this thousand-year period, the world will enjoy unprecedented peace and prosperity, and the world's population will recover from the tumultuous events that preceded Christ's reign.

> I saw the souls of those who had been beheaded for their testimony about Jesus. . . . They all came to life again, and they reigned with Christ for a thousand years.
>
> Revelation 20:4 NLT

> When the thousand years are up, Satan will . . . talk them into going to war. . . . They'll no sooner get there than fire will pour out of Heaven and burn them up.
>
> Revelation 20:7–9 MSG

During this time, human history will continue. Men and women will still be married, and they will welcome children into their families. Several generations will experience the blessing of living on the earth under the reign of Jesus as the earthly Lord. The Bible furthermore reveals that all people who go to the temporary heaven prior to the end-time events will return with Jesus. They will rule upon the earth with him during the one thousand years of his earthly reign. The people physically born and living during that time will experience a unique understanding of Jesus and recognize him as God's Messiah. They, too, will be required to place faith in him as God's Messiah to experience eternity in heaven with God.

At the end of one thousand years, the Bible says that Satan will be released from the Abyss and loosed upon the earth from his chains. Remarkably, Satan will scour the earth and successfully recruit a multitude of people who will willingly oppose Jesus in a final battle. While it is difficult to fathom how or why any person would choose to deny the loving authority of Jesus, particularly while experiencing the benefit of living under his reign, many people will do so. In an act of self-determination, they will align themselves with Satan as adversaries against God and seek to win in a final war against God.

This ultimate conflict is known popularly as Armageddon because of the prediction of its taking place in the area of Megiddo in Northern Israel. The biblical prophecies reveal that the world's armies that are under satanic authority will gather in this region to make war against God. The Bible says that this evil army will number "like the sand in the desert" and will be too numerous to be counted. They will surround Jerusalem with the intent to destroy it and all of God's people. However, in a final act of unparalleled might, God will rain fire down from heaven upon these warring forces, obliterating them en masse.

The battle is perceived to be apocalyptic in nature, meaning that it will bring about the end of the world as it is currently known and understood. In a larger sense, the word *apocalypse* means "an unveiling." This broader understanding of the apocalyptic nature of Armageddon reveals that this final battle will inaugurate the beginning of eternity, signified by the judgments of God over the faithful and the faithless populations of human history.

Following the divine intervention of God against the immense army of Satan, God will bind him and cast him eternally into the lake of fire. With Satan dispatched, God will commence with the final judgment upon the earth where the actions of all people will be judged. The people who neglected, ignored, or refused God's offer will be judged by their actions. Their rebellion and disobedience will not be forgiven and must be punished. These unfortunate souls will be cast into the lake of fire alongside Satan, the Antichrist, and the False Prophet. The people who had placed their faith in Jesus as Lord while living the physical life will be forgiven of their rebellion and offenses against God and will be given entry into the eternal heaven.

> Anyone whose name wasn't written in the book of life was thrown into the lake of fire.
>
> Revelation 20:15 CEV

Digging Deeper

Some people disagree with a literal interpretation of the prophetic events revealed in the Bible's book of Revelation. They argue that the events depicted are representative, symbolic, or metaphorical, rather than literal promises that will play out exactly as presented. While only God knows exactly what the future will reveal, it is important to realize that all Christian disciples agree on the final details that Jesus will claim victory over sin, evil, and rebellion. He will judge all people, and he will reign in heaven forever with those he has saved from hell.

Points to Remember

- Jesus will reign on the earth for one thousand years as a kind, perfect earthly ruler. The earth will be at peace during this time.

  - At the end of the earthly reign of Jesus, Satan will deceive a multitude of people, and these people will form a vast army to oppose God in a final battle.

- God will destroy this rebelling army, defeat Satan, and usher in the final judgment that will launch the endless time of eternity.

Check Your Understanding

- **Why does Jesus return to the earth?**

Jesus returns to the earth to rule upon it as the global King for one thousand years of unequaled peace and prosperity.

- **Why is Satan unleashed at the end of the one thousand years?**

The release of Satan at the end of the thousand-year reign of Christ demonstrates the rebellious nature of every person who does not have a restored relationship with God through faith in Jesus.

- **What is the final judgment that takes place after Jesus' victory in Armageddon?**

The final judgment is where God will judge the actions of everyone throughout history and determine whether they will spend eternity in hell apart from him or in heaven in his presence.

The Punishment of Satan

Once Satan has been defeated in the final battle of Armageddon, his eternal judgment awaits. The Bible details those last moments of earthly existence for Satan as well as his final condemnation. These definitive statements clarify that Satan will ultimately be defeated and that he cannot stand against the God who created him. These promises give hope and assurance. God's love is expansive, and his power to complete what he promised is unequaled. He will restore the relationship with his people that Satan broke when he deceived Adam and Eve.

The mistaken view of Satan that has continued through history is that when God ushers in the onset of eternity Satan will be the tyrannical overseer of hell. The Bible says, however, that after Satan is defeated at the battle of Armageddon, he will be cast into the fiery pits of hell alongside the Antichrist and the False Prophet. Then, in the process of the final judgment, God will throw hell itself into the eternal lake of fire. This pit of darkness will be forever separated from heaven, and imprisonment in it is irrevocable and everlasting.

The lake of fire is the eternal hell where all residents will be separated from God. This includes the legions of demons who were initially expelled from heaven and for whom this fiery destination was created. Satan will be tormented

This is the way our Savior God wants us to live. He wants not only us but everyone saved, you know, everyone to get to know the truth we've learned

1 Timothy 2:3–4 MSG

He, when He comes, will convict the world concerning sin and righteousness and judgment . . . and concerning judgment, because the ruler of this world has been judged.

John 16:8, 11 NASB

in this lake of burning sulfur forever, and he will be consumed by his murderous hate for God. The lake of fire will also imprison the spirits of the sad people who never trusted God or responded to his free offer of restoration and reconciliation. Together, these eternally lost souls will wail in lament over being separated from God, Satan among them, and certainly not as overseer.

Points to Remember

- Satan will be an inmate in hell and the lake of fire, not an overseer. He will be confined there forever.

- It is a tragedy for any human to go to hell. God desires all humans to accept his offer of restoration and go to heaven for eternity.

Check Your Understanding

- **Why is it important to understand Satan's destiny?**

It is important to understand Satan's destiny so that he is not incorrectly perceived to be the overseer of hell. He will suffer in eternal hell as one who has rejected God's love.

- **What does it mean that the imprisonment in the lake of fire is irrevocable and everlasting?**

This means that whoever is imprisoned in hell for acts of unforgiven rebellion and disobedience will be there forever. No being, human or demonic, can ever escape the tormenting, isolated confines of hell. No person should want to go to this horrible place.

FAQ—Is Satan Really Real?

A notorious movie villain once said, "The greatest trick the devil ever pulled was convincing the world he didn't exist." Many people either believe he doesn't exist or believe he exists but misunderstand his destructive ways. Some people imagine the devil as the tiny, red, pitchfork-wielding sprite sitting atop a person's shoulder whispering temptations. Some people think of him as a larger-than-life demon who rules over hell with dripping fangs and razor-sharp talons. These caricatures only mythologize the reality of Satan.

As a fallen angel destined for eternal confinement in the lake of fire, Satan is a spiritual being who roams the earth to oppose God. The Bible faithfully reveals Satan's influence and involvement in numerous acts of rebellion and disobedience. He instigated the initial disobedience of Adam and Eve. He was behind the calamity that befell Job. He deceived King David to inappropriately take a census of Israel, against God's command. He is pictured making accusations against Israel's high priest Joshua.

When the wicked one appears, Satan will pretend to work all kinds of miracles, wonders, and signs.

2 Thessalonians 2:9 CEV

The God of peace will soon crush Satan under your feet.

Romans 16:20 NLT

Satan is not simply an Old Testament invention to represent evil. Jesus reported that he saw Satan cast from heaven at the dawn of creation. While sojourning through the desert, Jesus withstood a three-wave attack from Satan when Satan attempted to thwart Jesus from launching his ministry. Jesus easily recognized Satan's presence behind the selfish motives of people. Jesus was always aware of the reality of Satan in the world, and he regularly warned his followers to be on the watch for Satan. The Gospels report that Satan possessed Judas to betray Jesus.

The Bible further reports that the early church was vigilant to safeguard against Satan's deceptive efforts to destroy lives and ruin the church. In several of his letters to people and to churches, Paul exhorted them to resist Satan's evil tricks. John told of the future vision where Satan is defeated, bound, and cast into the eternal lake of fire.

Points to Remember

- Satan is real. Despite myths that either minimize his abilities or expand his powers, Satan is a real spiritual being existing on this physical realm who continually strives to deceive humans.

- God wants people to be aware of Satan's reality and to take the necessary steps to guard against his temptations.

Check Your Understanding

- **Why is it important to understand the reality of Satan?**

It is important to understand the reality of Satan so that you can recognize when Satan is at work in your life, trying to deceive you to destroy your relationship with God.

- **How is Satan an essential part of God's plan?**

Satan is an essential part of God's plan because he is the one responsible for causing the broken relationship between God and humans. He tried and failed to rule and kill Jesus. He will be defeated and punished forever.

FAQ—What Are Satan's Limitations?

It is a mistake to think that Satan is God's evil counterpart. Some people even think that Satan is the opposite of God, perhaps even a god himself. The Bible reveals, however, that Satan is a created being and is limited in his power, influence, reach, and effectiveness. He is by no means an equal opposite to God. God's majesty and power are unmatched.

✳

Satan pales in comparison to God in every important measure. God knows everything, but Satan is limited in his knowledge. God is omnipresent, but Satan can be in only one place at one time. God is all-powerful, but Satan's power, while impressive, is limited. God's love and goodness have no limits. Satan's wickedness is limited to what he can accomplish in the short time before his final judgment.

Satan's abilities are often exaggerated because he is so misunderstood. It is important to remember that one-third of all the angels were cast from heaven, so a demonic realm does exist on the earth. However, just as Satan is limited intellectually, geographically, and influentially, so, too, are his demonic colleagues. Satan and his demons often receive undeserved credit for rebellion and disobedience that should rightfully be attributed to the humans involved.

Lord, there is no one like you! For you are great, and your name is full of power.

Jeremiah 10:6 NLT

No, in all these things we are more than victorious through Him who loved us.

Romans 8:37 HCSB

While it is important not to exaggerate the reality of Satan in the world, it is also important not to minimize his reality. The Bible is clear that Satan's influence on this world is real. At the same time, the Bible is also clear that Satan cannot kill or overcome a Christian. A demon cannot possess or relentlessly oppress any person who puts faith in Jesus as Lord. Christians face difficulties in the physical life, but God's promise is victory over Satan and the world.

Points to Remember

- Satan cannot be in more than one place at one time. His powers have limits. He is no match for God.

- God's plan is that Christians have freedom from satanic attacks and experience victory over Satan.

Check Your Understanding

- **Why is it essential to understand the limits of Satan's abilities?**

Understanding Satan's limited abilities is essential to avoid dismissing him as irrelevant or crediting him unnecessarily for evil deeds that are not the work of his hands.

- **What is important for a Christian to remember about Satan's power over the Christian?**

It is important to understand that Satan has little power over a Christian. He cannot kill a Christian, he cannot oppress a Christian, and he cannot overcome a Christian.

Hell—Real, Hot, and Hopeless

Every person is born with a natural orientation leading toward hell but is individually powerless to change course. Knowing the truth about hell is important to avoid this horrible destination.

Contents

The Reality of Hell 193

The Isolation of Hell 195

The Endlessness of Hell 197

FAQ—When Did God Create Hell? 199

FAQ—Why Did God Create Hell? 201

FAQ—Who Is in Hell? 203

FAQ—Is Hell a Literal Lake of Fire? 207

FAQ—Who Is the Overseer of Hell? 211

How will you escape the judgment of hell?

Matthew 23:33 NLT

The Reality of Hell

As incredible as heaven promises to be, the Bible also speaks of the reality of hell, which awaits everyone who refuses God's redemption and forgiveness. Throughout history, people have tried to deny the existence of hell by allegorizing biblical passages or by philosophizing that the current earth is in a hellish existence. Unfortunately, these efforts have been effective. Even so, hell is real. Anyone who hopes to avoid this despairing situation needs to understand its reality.

God designed hell as a prison to punish the league of angels who rebelled alongside Lucifer. God expelled all those fallen angels from the heaven of heavens to the realm of the second heaven, with the eventual, inevitable plan to confine them in the lake of fire. This is the original intent of hell, and God will fulfill this intent as planned.

> The LORD gives both death and life; he brings some down to the grave but raises others up.
>
> 1 Samuel 2:6 NLT
>
> It is better for you to lose one part of your body than for your whole body to be thrown into hell.
>
> Matthew 5:29 NLT

The gates of heaven, however, were opened to receive human occupants because of the human rebellion that took place on earth. Because every person is born predisposed to oppose God, every person is born with a destiny that is oriented toward hell. The path of the normal life leads to hell because every person, being human, offends and rebels against God. The only hope for a person is to be reoriented to humanity's original destination of heaven.

The Bible records that Jesus spoke more about hell than he did about heaven. He described it repeatedly as a place of torment, of weeping, and of despair. He spoke of its eternal, perpetual flames of judgment. He spoke of it in cautionary terms, exhorting people to understand that it is real and not a place to be dismissed. Jesus wanted everyone to know that God did not want even one person to go to hell, and he freely offered heaven to anyone who would accept it.

Points to Remember

- Hell is real. It is not an allegory or a philosophy. It is a physical destination that is described as a place of torment, unrelenting judgment, darkness, and sorrow.

- Hell was created for the fallen angels, not humans. People are sent to hell for their rebellious nature.

Check Your Understanding

- **What are some futile ways people try to dismiss the reality of hell?**

Some people deny the reality of hell despite the evidence pointing to its reality. Others speak of hell in allegorical terms or suggest that hell is simply the present reality on earth.

- **Why is it important to understand the reality of hell?**

God wants people to know that hell is a real, horrible place. Understanding hell's reality helps a person appreciate what God offers.

The Isolation of Hell

Hell is a paradoxical domain. Jesus taught that the path that leads to hell's destruction is wide and that many people will walk it. In fact, he made a point to mention that some people who call themselves followers of his will one day find themselves in hell because even though they did many kind deeds in the name of Jesus, they never had faith in him. For everyone who enters hell, regardless of the life that preceded this judgment, the afterlife will be immensely, intensely isolated and despairingly lonesome.

Traditional images of hell range from people being tormented by demons to legions of human slaves being forced to endlessly stoke the flames of the lake of fire. While these imaginations are evocative, they are not rooted in the Bible.

In comparing Lazarus to the wealthy man who died, one of the striking details of the man's plight was his profound awareness of his loneliness. He spoke of his desire that God warn his living brothers about the reality of hell. He was suddenly and eternally aware that he did not want anyone else that he knew and loved to experience what he was experiencing. While the adage suggests that "misery loves company," the wealthy man's experience reveals that hell is so abjectly miserable that nobody in hell wants anyone else to

I have five brothers, and I want him to warn them so they don't end up in this place of torment.

Luke 16:28 NLT

If anyone does not remain in me, he is like a branch that is thrown away and withers; such branches are picked up, thrown into the fire and burned.

John 15:6 NIV

have to suffer it. For the person who is assigned to hell due to selfishness, this benevolence is an even more profound revelation.

The wealthy man's lament also indicates that he had full awareness of his great separation from God. That separation is represented by an impassable chasm. This chasm, an expanse pictured in the physical life, is a real divide separating God and humans. People cannot overcome it on their own, so God did it for them. For those in hell, however, the opportunity to have this chasm bridged has been lost, and much of those people's eternal sorrow is the everlasting observation of what they will never experience with God.

Points to Remember

• Hell is so intensely tormenting that no person will want anyone else to experience its misery, not his loved ones or his most disliked adversary. If they were able, those who are currently in hell would implore the living to choose God's love instead of his judgment.

• Those who are in hell apparently will be able to view heaven but never experience it. They will perpetually observe their own separation from God, which is a primary source of their eternal agony.

Check Your Understanding

▪ **What does it mean that a person in hell is isolated?**

While it may be impossible from a human perspective to number the people in hell, each person there will have no attention given to them by any other individual and will not desire to be joined in hell by any other person.

▪ **What is the significance of the great chasm separating heaven and hell?**

The great chasm separating heaven and hell is significant because it indicates the utter hopelessness for those in hell. They can never cross into God's loving presence.

The Endlessness of Hell

Just as the eternal heaven will be a new creation outside time the way it is currently understood, so, too, will be the lake of fire that awaits all people whose names are not recorded in the Book of Life. It is not known whether the future reality obliterates time or radically redefines it with as-yet-undiscovered dimensions. Nevertheless, the current ability to comprehend the depth, breadth, width, vastness, and timelessness of hell only begins to address the despair that will overwhelm and forever occupy its residents.

The complexity of hell's eternity is not spelled out in the Bible in a comprehensive manner. However, a few comments regarding the experience in hell reveal interesting facts about the measurement of eternity's progress. The Bible says that those who rebel against God by worshiping the Antichrist in end times will experience the fullness of God's wrath. Their torment in the flames of the lake of fire will be forever, and they will have no rest day or night (Revelation 14:11). This does not mean that hell will have day and night in the conventional sense. In fact, the Bible declares that the blackest, never-ending darkness has been reserved for hell's occupants.

[These men are] wandering stars for whom is reserved the blackness of darkness forever.

Jude 1:13–14 NKJV

If anybody is preaching to you a gospel other than what you accepted, let him be eternally condemned!

Galatians 1:9 NIV

However, it is possible this means that even in hell, there will be a marked progression throughout the endless future.

For some people in the present physical reality, the passage of day into night means that an ongoing trial or tribulation has the possibility of ending. In hell, however, the passage of time offers no hope that the calamity will end. In hell, all agony is endless. There is no respite for those who suffer. There is only the acute awareness that forever marches onward, and in this horribly self-imposed prison, there is no possibility of escape, pardon, or parole.

Points to Remember

• Just as the new heaven will exist outside time and space, so, too, will the lake of fire. However the dimensions of eternity are measured, this place of everlasting judgment will house the condemned in perpetual punishment.

• The eternal hell appears to be able to mark the progress of time that will never end, which will cause every moment in the fiery Abyss to be interminably unbearable for its occupants.

Check Your Understanding

▪ **How is time in eternity different from time in the physical life?**

If time exists in eternity, its measurement is not a matter of progression toward the conclusion of God's redemptive plan. Time in eternity may serve the purpose of indicating the ongoing progress of forevermore.

▪ **How does time in the new heaven differ from time in the lake of fire?**

While the citizens of heaven will have forever to explore the unending vastness of God's love, the denizens of hell will perpetually churn in the grief of God's enduring wrath against their obstinacies.

FAQ—When Did God Create Hell?

Scholars and theologians are divided about the origin of hell. The Bible doesn't say when God created hell. Some clues can be found, however, that give some insight. The creation of hell is problematic for many Christians because of its torturous characteristics. By exploring how and when hell was started, we can gain a better understanding of why God made hell and, at the same time, gain insight into his holiness and the perfection of his plan.

The Bible declares in its opening sentence that God created the heavens and the earth "in the beginning" of time. No explicit reference to hell or the grave is made in the creation account. In Matthew 25:41, however, Jesus revealed that hell was created exclusively for Satan and his fallen angels and not for humans. Humans who rebel against God, however, will also be confined there along with the rebellious angels.

The biblical account of the first humans introduces Adam and Eve to Satan, embodied in a serpent. Satan had already been cast down from heaven and sentenced to the lake of fire. In the context of this judgment, Satan launched his assault on humans, leading them to disobedience and separation from God. Inferring from what is revealed in the Scriptures, it appears that God created hell at some point following the creation of angels—after the creation of heaven and the earth—and some time before the creation of Adam and Eve.

Do not fear those who kill the body but are unable to kill the soul; but rather fear Him who is able to destroy both soul and body in hell.

Matthew 10:28 NASB

Then the sea gave up its dead, and Death and Hades gave up their dead; all were judged according to their works.

Revelation 20:13 HCSB

Tragically, many humans do not choose the restoration God offers. Instead, they opt to remain outside God's redemptive love. They will spend eternity in a punitive realm that was designed for God's enemies, not his children. Even in this, God's creation is understood as "good" because this necessary consequence honors God's holiness. God does not desire for even one person to be in hell, but he respects every human's choice to accept or reject his offer of salvation.

Points to Remember

• The time line of hell's creation is not explicitly detailed in the Bible, but its reality is unquestioned. By exploring the biblical evidence, it appears that hell was created in response to the satanic rebellion but before the creation of humans.

• Hell's existence is in accordance with God's good will because it speaks to God's rightful judgment against disobedience and rebellion.

Check Your Understanding

▪ **Why is it important that God created hell before he created Adam and Eve?**

It is important that God created hell before Adam and Eve because if hell's creation followed human creation, it would mean that God created hell for humans as well as for the fallen angels.

▪ **What does it mean that God respects every person's choice to accept or reject his offer of salvation?**

The unfortunate reality that many people die and go to hell demonstrates that God's love is offered to all but mandated to none.

FAQ—Why Did God Create Hell?

Many people cannot understand how a loving God would banish his precious children to a place such as hell. The very notion of such an action seems cruel and excessive. These problematic thoughts are the result of a misunderstanding about why hell exists. Viewing hell as a torture chamber for God's children is a misrepresentation of why God created this harsh, isolated domain. Instead, hell should be understood by its biblical teaching as a punitive prison for those created beings who oppose God and seek to overthrow his reign as eternity's Lord.

⁂

Jesus revealed that hell was the place God had prepared for the fallen angel Lucifer and his rebellious comrades. Skeptics and cynics may interpret this either as a correction to a mistake by an imperfect God or as a severe reaction by a tyrannical, threatened God. These incorrect accusations against God continue when people learn that hell is also the destination for any person who chooses to reject God's offer of salvation through faith in Jesus.

> Depart from me, you who are cursed, into the eternal fire prepared for the devil and his angels.
>
> Matthew 25:41 NIV
>
> The one who rejects you, rejects me. And rejecting me is the same as rejecting God, who sent me.
>
> Luke 10:16 MSG

In reality, all these understandings fall short of the preemptive action undertaken by the holy God. He knew ahead of time about the satanic rebellion, and he prepared a place for the perpetrators. He knew that part of the satanic rebellion would result in the temptation and corruption of humanity. Because of this corruption, people would possess a flawed nature like Satan and oppose God. Accordingly, opposing God required a punitive judgment. God cannot violate his holy nature, so hell serves as the unfortunate destination for any created being who determines in his spirit to oppose God.

A common argument is that God is to blame for subjecting humans to the satanic temptation that resulted in human disobedience. This ignores the reality that humans choose to oppose God in countless ways every day. The Bible warns that those who oppose God are identified as "sons of the devil" and will share in the judgment awaiting him.

Points to Remember

- Hell was made for all created beings who choose to oppose God rather than to obey him. This opposition is reflected in a refusal to accept God's holy love.

- Man is guilty for choosing to oppose God. The consequence of this guilt is banishment to the realm created for the devil and his angels.

Check Your Understanding

- **Why did God have to create hell?**

God created humans and angels as eternal beings. Humans and angels who rebel against God will live forever in a prison of isolation apart from him as the judgment against their rebellion.

- **Why do people futilely attempt to blame God for hell?**

Part of the flawed, rebellious nature of humans is to blame God for the guilt of their offenses against him. This effort denies the responsibility every person faces for the disobedience each commits against God.

FAQ—Who Is in Hell?

Hell will be filled with people who missed, forsook, or neglected the opportunities they were given in the physical life to receive God's gift of forgiveness and to gain heaven. Just as is true for heaven, there will be surprises (from a human perspective) about who will be in hell, as well as about who will not be there. However, hell is going to be the residence not only of forsaken people, but it also promises to be the final home of torment of some of history's most notorious personalities and of the Bible's most dangerous creatures.

No one will be in hell who does not belong there. This is so even though every soul by human nature is born into a physical life that is oriented toward hell. Every person rebels against God, and it is only by the intervention of God that any person is delivered from hell. Those people who find themselves in hell have only themselves to blame—they rebelled against God and relied on themselves to establish a right standing before God. Every person who is or will be in hell will be found guilty of denying God, resisting him, and trusting in his or her own successes in an effort to win God's favor.

The devil . . . will be there with the beast and the false prophet, and they will be in pain day and night forever and ever.

Revelation 20:10 CEV

Anyone whose name was not found inscribed in the Book of Life was hurled into Lake Fire.

Revelation 20:15 MSG

The Bible lists general classifications of people who will find themselves in hell. This list includes people who are guilty of lies, violence, sexual immorality, and idolatry. This list, though not comprehensive, indicates the actions that, if not reconciled, will result in eternal condemnation. If a person's faith in Jesus does not identify him, his actions of rebellion and disobedience will.

The Bible does name some historical people who have been judged to eternal punishment. The Bible indicates that the pharaoh, the opposer of Moses, will receive God's wrath. The Bible also labels Judas, the betrayer of Jesus, as "a son of perdition." This means that because he fell into rebellion against God by his lust for money, power, and recognition, he consigned himself to an eternal judgment of God's wrath. With numerous other examples of people, families, and even entire nations who opposed God, the understated but clear principle is that rebellion against God that in any way is not reconciled by God's forgiveness results in inevitable and eternal banishment to hell.

While the identity of historic, biblical personalities is provocative, the Bible also promises that notorious future personalities are no less so. Two such people destined to hell are the Antichrist and the False Prophet. The Antichrist is a future human being of great influence, power, and persuasion who establishes himself as the future leader and attempts to fill the role of Messiah. He will deceive many, and he will be a man of terrible destruction. His cohort is a world leader called the False Prophet, a religious leader who successfully convinces many people to worship the Antichrist as God. These two people will be under satanic influence but will be guilty of their own offenses. They will be cast into hell for their acts.

Humans will not be the sole residents of hell. The Bible promises that Satan and his fallen demonic angels will also be consigned to the lake of fire for all eternity. The biblical evidence indicates they are aware of this inevitability and seek only to delay it from occurring as long as possible. Prior to their banishment into the lake of fire, they will be bound to the lower realms of heaven and earth. The fallen angels appear to be geographically limited to where they can wreak havoc, but some will be released to do great harm. In this, God will use them to execute judgment upon the world for its disobedience and rebellion. At some time in the future, all the rebellious angels who have been dispatched from the highest heaven will be cast into hell where they will not reign but will lament.

In addition to the fallen angels and the rebellious humans, other mysterious creatures are mentioned in the Bible as being residents of hell

> Then Death and Hades were cast into the lake of fire. This is the second death.
>
> Revelation 20:14 NKJV

released upon the earth as expressions of God's wrath against the rebellious. The Bible speaks of locustlike, armor-plated, scorpion-tailed, horse-faced creatures that will ascend from hell in a cloud of smoke that covers the skies to torment the people who oppose God. They are hellish creatures said to be under the authority of Apollyon, a synonym for Satan.

Digging Deeper

Four of the most notorious and mysterious personalities from the book of Revelation are the four horsemen of the Apocalypse mentioned in Revelation 6. Widespread disagreement and rampant speculation mark the incomplete understanding of these intriguing agents of God's judgment. Most scholars agree that these horses and their riders are symbolic personalities. The

horsemen are commonly understood to represent the deadly reign of the Antichrist (white horse), global war (red horse), global inflation and starvation (black horse), and global sickness, plagues, and death (pale horse).

Points to Remember

- Hell's occupants will include notorious figures from past world history, figures from future world calamity, and demons who have opposed God from the dawn of time, alongside common people who denied and defied God throughout their physical lives.

- All the eternal residents of hell will be tormented in the lake of fire. Neither Satan nor his demons will rule hell as authorities or punishers; they will join in the misery and suffering of being separated from God's love.

Check Your Understanding

- **Why does God place humans in a place of punishment that was designed for the rebellious angels?**

God places humans in hell because their rebellion is not unlike the rebellion of the fallen angels. The disobedience of humans is an offense to God's holiness, and if it cannot be forgiven it must be judged.

- **Why is it important to understand that the fallen angels will be tormented in hell?**

It is important to understand the fallen angels' inevitable punishment to have an accurate understanding of their future in the lake of fire. These demons will not torture humans in hell, but everyone will be in agony alike.

- **What is important to remember about the demonic locusts that ascend from hell?**

It is important to recognize that God will use these mysterious creatures to ravage humanity. This is a judgment of God in the future against rebellion on the earth.

FAQ—Is Hell a Literal Lake of Fire?

Many creative people throughout the centuries have tried to imagine the desolate, agonizing atmosphere of hell as the home of the condemned. Artists, writers, poets, and musicians have used a variety of resources to create the terrible imagery of a place where there is no good, no God, and an abundance of woe. Consequently, the collective understanding of hell is not entirely biblical and the actual environment may not appear as some have imagined it. However, from the extensive details shared through biblical descriptions, the vivid portrait of hell is striking in its hopeless expanse and torturous surroundings.

Jesus spoke often of hell in a cautionary way to show people God's better plan. He wanted his audiences to have a sense of the horror of hell so they would make the choice to receive the gift of heaven that he offered to them. He spoke of hell candidly, and from those conversations people of every generation have gained insight to what awaits those who die to the physical life without faith in Jesus.

In sharing the account of the wealthy man and Lazarus, Jesus pointed to several revealing aspects of hell's environs. First, hell is described as a place of torment and as a place of agony. Those confined to the prison of hell will find it to be a terrible environment because they will be acutely aware of their eternal separation from God. They will suffer the perpetual, relentless understanding that they squandered the opportunity to forever be in the presence of the perfect, loving, holy God. They will fully comprehend

> The LORD will swallow them up in His wrath, and fire will devour them.
>
> Psalm 21:9 NASB
>
> The Son of Man will send forth His angels, and they will . . . throw them into the furnace of fire; in that place there will be weeping and gnashing of teeth.
>
> Matthew 13:41–42 NASB

that they chose to experience God's wrath rather than the fullness of God's love.

The term *torture* is problematic to modern readers because of the interpretation that for torture to occur, there must be someone or something that inflicts this torture upon the person in agony. However, there is no evidence in the Bible that indicates the presence of any such torturer. In fact, as the wealthy man's own account indicates, hell appears to be a place of extreme isolation. The wealthy man was tormented by his endless thirst, and he asked God to send Lazarus down to dip his finger in water that it would cool his parched tongue. He did not indicate awareness of any other person who might otherwise have provided this service to him. This doesn't mean that each person is placed in an individual hell; rather, it intimates that even in hell a person is solely focused on himself, just as he was in the physical life. While hell is populated with innumerable independent-minded people, none of them appear to focus upon anything apart from a personal eternal plight.

Other terminology used to describe hell gives indication to its bleak setting. It is described numerous times as "the outer darkness." This means that it is a place that is separated from the light of God's holiness and the warmth of God's love. The intense awareness of this isolation and dark, everlasting existence no doubt is profoundly overwhelming. Jesus repeatedly mentioned hell as a place of "weeping and gnashing of teeth." This means that hell is a place of total sadness as well as a place of unimaginable self-loathing and anger. The imagery presented is of a person so self-consumed in hell that he perpetually grinds his teeth in steel-jawed rage while eternally agonizing in weeping, all-encompassing grief over his never-ending predicament.

Finally, hell itself will be thrown into the eternal lake of fire. The Bible speaks of hell as a place of flames. This is the final destination of Satan and all the fallen angels. The Antichrist will be there, as will the False Prophet. None of these enemies of God will reign there. All will join in the suffering and lament, along with all the humans who rejected the

Tie him up hand and foot, and throw him into the outer darkness, where there will be weeping and gnashing of teeth.

Matthew 22:13 HCSB

love of God in the physical life. It is in the lake of fire that these people will experience what the Bible calls "the second death." This eternal experience following the white throne judgment of Jesus Christ is the final, unending judgment of God's wrath upon disobedience and rebellion.

Digging Deeper

Many people believe that "the second death" speaks of the idea that as a final act of wrath following the white throne judgment, God will annihilate, or utterly destroy, the souls of people whose names are not written in the Book of Life. The belief is that casting these people into the lake of fire is the act that will destroy them. However, there is no scriptural support that "the second death" is an act of destruction; rather, it is biblically consistent to interpret it as an eternal act of judgment where the death is the spiritual, eternal separation from God.

Points to Remember

- Hell is populated by countless souls, but there is no community or fellowship there. Every person is isolated and self-absorbed in tormented regret.

- Hell is burning hot with the flames of God's judgment, but it is also utterly dark in the absence of God's love and righteousness.

- Hell itself will be condemned to eternal judgment in the lake of fire, where all rebellion and disobedience against God will be punished forever.

Check Your Understanding

- **Why is hell called "the outer darkness"?**

Hell is called "the outer darkness" because it is a place that God has created completely apart from his love and holiness. It is the only place in eternity from which he has utterly separated himself.

- **Why is it important to understand the lake of fire as a literal destination?**

Attempts to allegorize hell and the lake of fire can lead a person to minimize the harsh reality that awaits those who rebel against God. Appreciating hell and the lake of fire as literal destinations helps a person understand the magnitude of God's offer of salvation.

- **What does it mean that hell is a place of "weeping and gnashing of teeth"?**

The agony of hell is a place of immense sorrow and self-hating anger. Neither of these intense emotions will cease or even relent in hell.

- **Will the devil reign in hell?**

Hell is the final destination of the devil, but he won't reign there or have any kind of jurisdiction. Satan, all the fallen angels, the Antichrist, and the False Prophet will all be there together, but they will all join in the suffering and lament.

FAQ—Who Is the Overseer of Hell?

The common perception among people who believe in the reality of heaven and hell is that Satan is in charge of hell. Logically, it makes sense that God's adversary would oversee the place where the people go who oppose God. Legendary tales have supported this widely accepted myth. Countless jokes include the premise that Satan is hell's landlord. While Satan does have great power, his relationship with hell is not one that he is eager to experience. So, if Satan is not hell's overseer, who is? Many are surprised by the biblical truth that Jesus Christ is.

Hell appears to be a gated community and is a prison for those who oppose God and rebel against him. Currently upon the earth, Satan exercises significant power and impressive authority. When Jesus walked the earth, Satan brazenly confronted him and offered him earthly power and dominion if Jesus would simply submit to Satan's earthly authority. Jesus refused to give in to this offer and sent Satan away.

While it may make sense and be tempting to extend Satan's current authority on earth into a future authority over hell, there is no scriptural support of this notion. The Bible affirms that in the future, hell itself will be encompassed by the lake of fire. There, Satan will be

> I am the living one. I died, but look—I am alive forever and ever! And I hold the keys of death and the grave.
>
> Revelation 1:18 NLT

> From the very beginning, I told what would happen long before it took place. I kept my word.
>
> Isaiah 46:10 CEV

forever chained in the torment of God's judgment. When this happens, the effect of God's power over Satan will be finally and fully understood.

The fact that Satan will himself be bound and eternally imprisoned in the lake of fire demonstrates that he is by no means the administrator of hell. The Bible teaches that Jesus is Lord over hell.

Jesus acknowledged that he alone possesses the keys to death and hades. He is the author of life and death. He alone knows the end from the beginning, on an individual basis as well as on the universal scale. No being, no demon, no fallen angel can snatch these keys from Jesus. When Satan tempted Jesus, he was offering what Jesus already rightly possessed.

Even though Jesus revealed himself as the overseer of hell, he is not the hands-on administrator of torture and punishment. Because Jesus overcame the penalty of disobedience and overcame death, he rightfully demonstrated his authority over the realm of death. This is why hell is a place of everlasting punishment against those who rebel and not a dark place of hidden conspiracies of eventual overthrow. In hell, Jesus reigns as Lord, and every soul in this domain of damnation acknowledges his unimpeachable authority over all of creation.

Because Jesus is sovereign over hell, he is able to use it specifically for his purposes. The Bible reveals that Jesus will do so in the future. Jesus will allow the pit of hell to release a hideous swarm of hellish locusts to torment the rebellious humans still populating the earth. God will use every resource at his disposal to demonstrate his holiness and to execute his wrath against human unholiness.

At the great white throne judgment, Jesus will demonstrate the fullness of his authority over hell when he orders the temporary hell to be thrown into the lake of fire. At the conclusion of his judgment, Jesus will have brought all disobedience and rebellion into condemnation, he will have destroyed the current earth with a consuming flame, and he will have imprisoned all the fallen angels and mutinous humans in the darkest reaches of the eternal lake of fire. In his eternal reign over all creation, Jesus will be worshiped as Lord by all creation. Even the personalities in heaven will kneel and submit to his supreme authority. Their worship will be a never-ending pained act of confession of their own guilt.

Myth Buster

Disagreement and confusion abound over whether or not Jesus descended into hell following his death on the cross. The Apostles' Creed, a statement of belief that dates from about AD 400, is commonly used by several mainline churches, including Congregational, Episcopal, Lutheran, Methodist, Presbyterian, and Roman Catholic churches. The line "he descended into hell" occurs in traditional versions, but "he descended to the dead" occurs in other traditional versions. This is where the confusion occurs. The word *hell* is used to cover both the temporary hell and the permanent hell. Since the permanent hell, the lake of fire, is a future event, that's probably not what is meant. In the context of the Apostles' Creed, the word *hell* is generally considered to refer to the place of the dead, *sheol* in Hebrew and *hades* in Greek.

> I'll pay all people in full for their life's work. I'm A to Z the First and the Final, Beginning and Conclusion.
>
> Revelation 22:12–13 MSG

Points to Remember

- Jesus is the gatekeeper and key-holder to death and hell. He is in control of every aspect of life and death.

- Jesus' sovereignty over hell does not mean that Jesus is the administrator of hell. Hell is the prison for those who reject the lordship of Jesus while living in the physical realm.

Check Your Understanding

- **Why won't Satan be the administrator over hell?**

Satan won't be the administrator because he himself will be bound and eternally imprisoned in the lake of fire.

- **What does it mean that Jesus knows the end from the beginning?**

Only Jesus knows every detail of every life, as well as every detail of all life. He knows when a life begins and when it ends, and every detail in between. He is sovereign over all affairs of all human history as it moves forward toward his plan of redemption.

- **Why does it matter that Jesus can even use the demonic creatures in judging people?**

All creation above the earth, on the earth, and under the earth will submit to the authority of Jesus Christ. Every person will acknowledge Jesus as Lord, either in a song of praise or in a dirge of sorrow.

- **Why was Satan's temptation of Jesus ludicrous?**

When Satan tempted Jesus, he was offering what Jesus already rightly possessed.

You in the Afterlife

Heaven offers endless potential; however, the potential is possible only for those who would strive to lay claim to its wonderful possibilities. Discover what heaven avails to all people

Contents

Your Body in the Afterlife 217

Your Home in the Afterlife 221

Your Work in the Afterlife 223

Your Relationships in the Afterlife 225

Your Past and the Afterlife 229

Your Rewards in the Afterlife 231

Your Attitude in the Afterlife 235

FAQ—Will the Physical Effects of This Life Be
Evident in Eternity? 237

FAQ—Will I Mourn Loved Ones Not in Heaven? 239

FAQ—Will I Recognize My Friends and Family in Heaven? ... 243

FAQ—Will My Marriage and Family Relationships
Continue in Heaven? 245

FAQ—Will I Be Able to Ask God Questions? 247

FAQ—Will My Pets Be in Heaven? 249

FAQ—Will Heaven Be Boring? 251

You will know the truth, and the truth will make you free.

John 8:32 NASB

Your Body in the Afterlife

Medical professionals agree that a healthy body image is important. This means to think correctly about your physical body and not be unrealistic in your expectation of how your physical body should appear. In heaven, every human is promised a new eternal body that far surpasses the quality of their physical body. This new body is described in spectacular terms. Having a healthy image of this eternal body is important in imagining the exciting potential of heaven's reality.

The Bible describes current physical bodies as "weak," "corruptible," and "under the curse." These terms describe the physical limitations common to all people. In heaven, however, a person's soul is united with a new body that is unimpaired, incorruptible, and free from the curses of the physical life.

Heavenly bodies are free from disease, defect, and deficiency. Injuries sustained in the physical life will not hinder a person in eternity. Eyeglasses, contact lenses, hearing aids, and dental implants will no longer be needed. Wheelchairs, hospital beds, and prosthetics will be things of the earthly past. Because heaven is void of any jealousy, selfishness, or shame, heaven's physical bodies will reflect

So it is with the resurrection of the dead: Sown in corruption, raised in incorruption.

1 Corinthians 15:42 HCSB

You were slain, and purchased for God with Your blood men from every tribe and tongue and people and nation.

Revelation 5:9 NASB

individual beauty and perfection from the universal perspective of the Creator. Body features that a person may have been embarrassed about, ashamed of, or simply not happy with in the physical life will not be disappointing or distracting in heaven. There will be no desire for nose jobs or tummy tucks. For a person to have a perfect body in heaven means that either God will correct the body or he will correct the person's mistaken perception about his or her body.

While everyone will enjoy the flawlessness of their eternal body, the Bible indicates that individual bodies will appear similar to but different from the ones people had while living the physical life. After Jesus was resurrected from the tomb, he walked an extended distance with two disciples  who did not recognize him despite his intimate conversation with them. It was only in the disciples' upper room when they saw the wounds on his wrists and side that they recognized him. Later, Jesus appeared on the shores of Galilee while several of his most faithful disciples were out fishing on a boat. When the disciples saw him, they recognized him immediately. The implication of Jesus' own example is that humans will appear different. Eternal bodies will not have the physical limitations common to the temporary bodies of the physical life, but each person will still be unique and identifiable by the characteristics possessed in the physical life.

A predicament common to the temporary physical body is that it simply changes. Weight fluctuates according to different variables. People choose to undergo cosmetic surgery to alter their appearance. Some people decide to adorn their bodies with tattoos, piercings, or other modifications. Many women go through physical changes after childbirth, and many men discover that even as their hairlines recede, other changes begin to take place as well. In heaven, there will be no need for girdles, support hose, beauty appointments, or face-lifts. Furthermore, there will be no hearing aids, no eyeglasses, no braces or dentures, and no artificial knees or hips.

Much is unknown about how God will manifest the perfection he perceives in each person. No one in heaven will be disappointed in any way with the human form they receive for eternity. No one in heaven will have a body that gets tired or is inefficient. Jesus' example offers exciting hints. For instance, he demonstrated the ability to enter rooms with locked doors and travel long distances in unexplainably brief spans of time.

Heaven is a place of physical transformation, not conformation. This means that heaven will celebrate the diversity expressed in the world today. Heaven will comprise all the world's nationalities and races. However, all nations and races will share one common trait in heaven: every citizen of heaven will glow with the reflection of God's holy glory. Every person across the heavenly expanse will radiate this glow. Heaven's physical bodies will be eternal demonstrations of the perfect, intimate relationship that each person enjoys with God.

> Those who lead many to righteousness will shine like the stars forever.
>
> Daniel 12:3 NLT

Digging Deeper

While humans will be free from physical limitations in heaven, the Bible suggests Jesus may display the physical wounds sustained while living on the earth. Prior to his crucifixion, Jesus was whipped and beaten, had his beard pulled out, and had a crown of thorns pushed atop his head. He was nailed to the cross where he died. In the book of Revelation, he is described as a slain Lamb. If Jesus does indeed bear the scars of his wounds in heaven, it will be an eternal reminder of the extent of God's love.

Points to Remember

- God will give resurrected bodies that reunite people's physical being with their souls.

- Resurrected bodies will be free from the limitations that hinder people in the temporary physical reality.

- Everyone will be perfectly pleased with the bodies they receive.

Check Your Understanding

- **What does it mean that the human heavenly body is incorruptible?**

A human's heavenly body is incorruptible because it is not subject to sickness, disease, or death. It is not impaired or limited in any way.

- **Why is it important that the eternal body will be similar to the temporary earthly body?**

The similarity between the temporary earthly body and the eternal heavenly body is important because it reveals that each person will maintain his unique identity and individual personality in heaven.

- **What is the significance of the reflective glow that will be common to all humans in heaven?**

Every human will reflect the radiant glory of God's holiness in heaven. This aspect of the resurrected creation shows the intimate reunion between God and humans.

- **Will people get new bodies in heaven, or will their old bodies be fixed up?**

The Bible describes current physical bodies as "weak," "corruptible," and "under the curse." These bodies have limitations. In heaven, people will have new bodies that are unimpaired, incorruptible, and free from the curses of the physical life.

Your Home in the Afterlife

For the citizens of heaven, eternity promises to be an environment where life is fully experienced. This means that each person will not only have his home in heaven, but he will also have an individual home in heaven. Between Jesus' resurrection and second coming, he created homes specifically designed for everyone who would one day inhabit the heavenly realm. The dimensions of heaven as revealed in the Bible offer exciting possibilities of what these eternal dwellings have to offer.

Before Jesus was crucified, buried, and resurrected, he told his followers that he was leaving to prepare a place for them in heaven, where God had many "rooms" or "mansions." The message that Jesus conveyed with this encouragement was that a person's home in heaven would be a spacious individual dwelling that would be a part of the overall community of heaven. While heaven only knows whether these abodes will form neighborhoods or be part of a single immense creation of God, people can be certain that their homes in heaven will be made specifically for them to occupy.

Moreover, the homes in heaven will be places of interaction and celebration. No one will suffer from loneliness or have a desire to be isolated from the rest of heaven's commu-

In my Father's house are many rooms. . . . I am going there to prepare a place for you. . . . I will come back and take you to be with me that you also may be where I am.

John 14:2–3 NIV

Listen! I am standing and knocking at your door. If you hear my voice and open the door, I will come in and we will eat together.

Revelation 3:20 CEV

nity. Rather, your heavenly home will be a place where you will welcome others and enjoy one another's company in the presence of God. Your eternal calendar will be full of plans to enjoy laughter, real experiences, and even worship with the others whose home is in heaven.

Heaven is described as a place of immense dimensions. The apostle John did his best to explain heaven as a place where the streets and the city alike are made from gold so pure that it appears as glass, and the city gates are made from single pearls, reflecting gems. Whether a person's temporary earthly home is humble or extravagant, it cannot compare to the dwelling being prepared in heaven by Jesus.

Points to Remember

- Jesus assured his followers that his time in heaven prior to his return would be used to create a home for every citizen of heaven.

- Heaven's homes will serve as dwellings for its citizens and also as places for people to enjoy one another in the presence of God.

Check Your Understanding

- **What is the difference between your "place" in heaven and God's many "rooms"?**

God's many "rooms" indicate that he has made exactly as many dwellings as the number of people who will one day occupy heaven. Your "place" indicates that one such "room" is reserved for you as part of God's home in heaven.

- **Why does it matter that your home will be a place of community?**

It is significant that your home be a place of community because this promise is that you will enjoy the company of other people, angels, and even God himself in the friendly, personal environment of your eternal home.

Your Work in the Afterlife

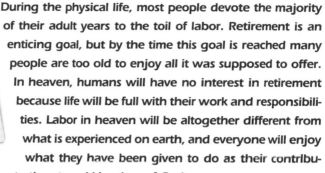

During the physical life, most people devote the majority of their adult years to the toil of labor. Retirement is an enticing goal, but by the time this goal is reached many people are too old to enjoy all it was supposed to offer. In heaven, humans will have no interest in retirement because life will be full with their work and responsibilities. Labor in heaven will be altogether different from what is experienced on earth, and everyone will enjoy what they have been given to do as their contribution to the eternal kingdom of God.

The fullness of what humans will do in heaven is unknown, but the Bible offers several clues to the exciting experience that awaits those who will go there. Several scriptural references refer to humans reigning with Christ over creation in eternity. The possibilities for this are intriguing. Humans will be delegated stewardship responsibility over the earth and even the universe once it has been re-created and united with the eternal heaven. The Bible declares that people will be rulers over the earth and will freely enter and depart from the gates of the New Jerusalem.

We are His workmanship, created in Christ Jesus for good works, which God prepared beforehand that we should walk in them.

Ephesians 2:10 NKJV

There will no longer be any curse; and the throne of God and of the Lamb will be in it, and His bond-servants will serve Him.

Revelation 22:3 NASB

The functional definition of *work* will be restored to its original meaning in heaven. One of the consequences of human rebellion on earth was that *work* became *toil*. However, in heaven a person's work will be the practical expression of a person's interests, passions, and joys. While some industries will be unnecessary—such as the funeral and medical industries—many pursuits that are valid in this life will be valid in the next life.

It is also not unreasonable to assume that eternity offers new careers that have not been yet explored. Regardless of personal rank or individual responsibility, the activities of heaven will be allocated to perfectly suit the perfect person. No one will ever tire or become bored in taking part in their heavenly responsibilities.

Points to Remember

- Every person will have responsibilities to fulfill in heaven. Everyone will have the authority necessary to complete their work without toil, and they will never tire of their efforts.

- Each person's work will be perfectly suited by God to the person.

Check Your Understanding

- **Why will work be better in eternity than it is now?**

Work in eternity will be better than it is on earth because in heaven work will not be toil. You will not grow weary doing the things you enjoy, and all your efforts will be meaningful, purposeful, and worshipful.

- **What does it mean that you will have authority in heaven?**

God promises that his children will reign with him over creation. This means you will have authority to accomplish God's objectives for you in a fully cooperative environment where everyone is perfectly suited to their assigned responsibilities.

Your Relationships in the Afterlife

The physical life is about starting and building relationships. From close family relationships with parents, siblings, and extended kin to the close relationships with friends, coworkers, and neighbors, relationships give meaning and add value to life's experiences. It is joyful when good friends or beloved family are reunited after extended times apart. While the nature of relationships changes in heaven, the importance and joy of them will be expressed in deeper and more meaningful ways than ever understood during the physical life. The idea of a family reunion takes on new meaning in heaven.

God created humans to have an eternal relationship with him. In the garden of Eden, God declared that it was not good for Adam to be alone, and so God created Eve to be his mate and to walk beside him. God's plan from the beginning was for humans to have deep, meaningful, and lasting relationships with other people, just as they were created to have a deep, meaningful, and lasting relationship with him. The Bible promises that relationships initiated on the earth during the physical life will continue in heaven for all people who share a common faith in Jesus as Lord.

There will be one huge family reunion with the Master.

1 Thessalonians 4:18 MSG

In this world they will be given a hundred times as many . . . brothers and sisters and mothers and children. . . . And in the world to come, they will have eternal life.

Mark 10:30 CEV

Before their fall into disobedience, Adam and Eve were united by God, and God commanded them to fill the earth with their offspring and descendants. Everyone who goes to heaven will be part of the singular family of God, but nothing in Scripture indicates that family relationships established on earth are invalidated in heaven. People's earthly relationships will be deeper and fuller in heaven when they are understood and appreciated in relationship to God.

While there won't be marriage in heaven as here on earth, there will be marriage between Christ and his church. What this means is that men and women who were married on the earth will enjoy a closeness that was established on earth but perfected in heaven. The earthly mind struggles to comprehend a relationship that surpasses and transcends the happiest marriage, but this is the promise of heaven.

Other family relationships will extend beyond the temporary physical life to the eternal life in heaven. The Bible indicates that because heaven is a place where the mind and spirit are made whole with an eternal body, every person will have a clear recall of all the people from their physical lives, and recognition will likely be an easier task in heaven than it is on earth.

The potential for how these reunions occur in heaven is overwhelming. There will be older generations of families who died before ever knowing their descendants. In heaven, they will reunite as heavenly citizens, recognizing one another and overjoyed to share a common identity as children of God.

Likewise, people from different ages and eras will be recognizable to others despite being separated by vast expanses of time and geographic location. The biblical account of Christ's transfiguration and meeting with Moses and Elijah in the presence of the apostles Peter, John, and James reveals that the disciples of Jesus recognized the resurrected identities of the ancient prophets despite living several centuries later. In heaven, Old Testament and New Testament personalities will be recognizable, as will notable Christians from history. While heaven is not a place where people will be omniscient in the same way God is all-knowing, people will nevertheless be more perceptive, more understanding, and more clear-thinking. Where introductions are necessary, they will take place without difficulty because there is no fear or negative feeling.

> Their eyes were opened and they recognized Him.
>
> Luke 24:31 NASB

Finally, friendships established on earth will continue in heaven, but without jealousy, disappointment, or other problems common in earthly relationships. Close friends will be even closer, and new friendships will form in eternity.

Dictionary

transfiguration *(n.)* a special event in biblical history when the earthly form of Jesus was changed to reveal his perfect, glorious, heavenly appearance.

Myth Buster

One mistaken concept about heaven is that eternity is only about an individual person being in the presence of God forever. While a person's individual relationship with God is the primary consideration of heaven, it is not the only relationship that matters. The Bible offers repeated encouragement that Christians will be in heaven together and that heaven will honor and extend the godly relationships established on earth in the full context of Christ's perfect relationship with all people in heaven.

Points to Remember

• Relationships that are established on earth will continue in heaven. Relationships such as marriage and family will have a different, perfect, and full context in light of the restored relationship every person will enjoy with God.

• People will recognize one another in heaven, even if their awareness of one another on earth was minimal. There will be new friendships and other relationships formed in heaven, too.

Check Your Understanding

▪ **How will marriage in heaven be different from marriage on earth?**

Marriage in heaven describes the complete union between Jesus and all Christians, while marriage on earth describes the intimate relationship between a man and a woman.

▪ **How will families in heaven be different from families on earth?**

Only family members who have put their faith in Jesus will be in heaven. Everyone who has done this will be part of one large family in heaven.

▪ **Why is it important to understand that relationships will continue in heaven?**

It is important to understand that relationships will continue because it shows that God's purpose is to continue in heaven what he created on earth as a blessing, and that he will correct and perfect the things on the earth that are good, but flawed or imperfect, such as human relationships.

Everybody makes mistakes. Usually, the mistakes are small, but sometimes they can be significant. Every mistake a person makes in life will be forgiven by God in order to allow that person into heaven. Most people hope that God will both forgive and forget all their mistakes and offenses. God's forgiveness allows people to fully worship God in heaven for who he truly is and for who they are because of him.

A common axiom in the attempt to forgive others is "forgive and forget." Rarely is such an aim ever actually accomplished. When people try to reconcile their need to be forgiven by God, they attempt to apply this same principle to God's remembrance of their offenses against him. While the Bible declares that God removes a person's offenses as far as the east is from the west, nowhere does the Bible suggest that God ever forgets human rebellion. In fact, the Bible says that God deliberately remembers those offenses no more. This powerful phrase does not mean that God forgets; rather, it means that God chooses not to judge people guilty for their wrong actions if they have sought forgiveness through faith in Jesus.

As far as the east is from the west, so far has He removed our transgressions from us.

Psalm 103:12 NKJV

It is I who sweep away your transgressions for My own sake and remember your sins no more.

Isaiah 43:25 HCSB

The Bible says that when people become Christian while in the earthly life, they are new creations who are perfectly loved and fully accepted by God. When the physical bodies die and people go to heaven, they do so as people whose offenses against God are forgiven and left behind in the physical body. Everything that is good and that God will bless will accompany the soul and spirit into heaven, where a perfect new beginning occurs. While a final judgment awaits Christians prior to the onset of heaven, it is a judgment of commendation and reward.

Points to Remember

• The mistakes made in the current physical life are totally forgiven if a person has a faith relationship with Jesus.

• God does not forget a person's offenses against him. Instead, he chooses not to hold the person guilty for having rebelled against God. This means that Jesus already paid the punishment.

Check Your Understanding

▪ **Why is it more powerful that God remembers rather than forgets a person's disobedience?**

If God were forgetful, he would not be all-knowing. It is a more power-ful evidence of God's knowledge that he chooses to forgive rather than to forget.

▪ **What does it mean that a person's offenses are "left behind" in a body that dies?**

For people who experience God's forgiveness, their offenses against God have already been accounted for by Jesus' sacrificial death. This means that these people will not be judged for those same offenses and forbidden entrance into heaven.

Your Rewards in the Afterlife

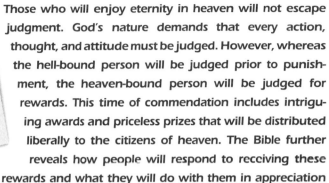

Those who will enjoy eternity in heaven will not escape judgment. God's nature demands that every action, thought, and attitude must be judged. However, whereas the hell-bound person will be judged prior to punishment, the heaven-bound person will be judged for rewards. This time of commendation includes intriguing awards and priceless prizes that will be distributed liberally to the citizens of heaven. The Bible further reveals how people will respond to receiving these rewards and what they will do with them in appreciation of God's unmatchable generosity.

After Jesus wins the final battle of world history against Satan and the people of the globe who oppose him, God will usher in the end of the present world and inaugurate eternity. Those who oppose God, deny him, or refuse his offer of forgiveness will have their actions judged and punished. They will be placed in the eternal lake of fire, forever separated from God. Immediately following this, people who trusted God, who believed in his promises to rescue them from the penalties of their rebellion, and who lived according to the faith that Jesus was God's plan to provide them entry into heaven will face an entirely different standard of judgment. These people are known as those whose names are written in the Book of Life, which apparently records the names of all history's people who will live in heaven forever.

Behold, I am coming soon! My reward is with me, and I will give to everyone according to what he has done.

Revelation 22:12 NIV

We must all stand before Christ to be judged. We will each receive whatever we deserve for the good or evil we have done in this earthly body.

2 Corinthians 5:10 NLT

Prior to entering this eternal existence of wonder and joy, every citizen will face a judgment of his or her life's conduct. Every detail from their lives will be scrutinized and judged by God. Heaven's citizens will face judgment so that their good conduct will be rewarded. Since God has promised that the penalty for all bad conduct has already been accounted for in the death and resurrection of Jesus, these offenses will be acknowledged as accounted for, and the person's good conduct will be rewarded.

Life's conduct being examined at this time—the rewards judgment— is determined to be good or bad based upon whether it was done as a response to faith in Jesus or as an act springing from a selfish motive. Even if an action was prompted by good intentions, if it was done by a person apart from God's initiative, God does not obligate himself to commend or reward it. However, everything done as a response to faith in Jesus will be rewarded, no matter how seemingly insignificant at the time.

The rewards in heaven will be allocated for any number of actions performed during the physical life. The apostle Paul mentioned that friends who follow him in heaven will be a crown given to him. This suggests that people who share their faith with others while living will enjoy commendation in the afterlife for this activity. The Bible also says that heaven's population will be given crowns of righteousness and authority as rewards. These crowns are actual bestowments of special authority and responsibility in the eternal kingdom for faithfulness expressed by a person during the physical life. God will richly reward those in heaven according to their ability to appropriately receive such honor from their Creator.

Interestingly, the Bible clearly teaches that all who receive such illustrious rewards will cast these crowns at the feet of Jesus in an authentic display of worship. This reverent action is a symbolic demonstration that acknowledges the eternal sovereignty of Jesus as Lord.

For the people who go to heaven, eternity will be marked by lavish rewards. Not only are these rewards crowns, titles, and authority, but also new and perfect bodies. The Bible also promises that God will give every person a new name that will be known to all. Heaven's citizenry

> God has something stored up for you in heaven, where it will never decay or be ruined or disappear.
>
> 1 Peter 1:4 CEV

will be clothed in righteousness, which suggests a wardrobe unlike anything fashioned on earth and certainly more dazzling than anything ever created. This is what the Bible promises: "All who are victorious will be clothed in white. I will never erase their names from the Book of Life, but I will announce before my Father and his angels that they are mine" (Revelation 3:5 NLT).

Finally, and most significant, every person is rewarded with heaven itself, and with the promise of being in the presence of God forever!

Digging Deeper

Some scholars disagree about when the rewards judgment will occur. Many hold to the view that it will occur after the tribulation, prior to the revelation of the permanent heaven. Others, though, believe that the rewards judgment for believers occurs immediately after a person dies and is resurrected. Still others reason that

the rewards judgment will be timed in relation to when Jesus rescues all believers from being persecuted by the Antichrist by removing them from the earth and placing them in heaven. Regardless of when the rewards judgment will actually occur, the fact that it will occur is indisputable.

Points to Remember

• Every person going to heaven will be judged before entering heaven. This judgment will strip away the things done in the physical life that didn't please God, but it will richly reward everything done as a response to the person's faith in Jesus.

• Among the treasures mentioned to be given to people include crowns, titles, authority, and responsibilities in heaven as well as new bodies, new names, new homes, and heaven to be enjoyed with God.

Check Your Understanding

■ **What does it mean that heaven's citizens will be rewarded with crowns in heaven?**

The reward of crowns in heaven means that people will be rewarded with authority and responsibility in heaven for the faithfulness to God they expressed during the physical life.

■ **What is significant about heaven's citizens' casting their rewarded crowns at the feet of Jesus?**

The act of casting their rewarded crowns at Jesus' feet acknowledges Jesus' eternal sovereignty over the heavenly creation.

■ **Why won't Christians be punished for their offenses against God?**

At the rewards judgment, the actions of Christians that were offenses against God will not be punished because those actions were already accounted for by Jesus.

Your Attitude in the Afterlife

Character flaws and personal peccadilloes are so common that they are often ignored, minimized, or apologized away. Jealousy, gossip, mean-spirited sarcasm, competitive attitudes, and general unpleasantness are all accepted and accommodated in the physical life. In heaven, however, there won't be any selfishness to compel a person to advance a personal agenda at the expense of others. What a difference this will be. People will be able to relate in unprecedented expressions of perfect love and cooperation.

It is difficult to imagine an existence where humans are totally cooperative and completely noncompetitive. It is hard to imagine what life will be like without jealousy, insecurity, anger, or selfishness. Yet this is the promise of heaven. In heaven, every person will be filled with gratitude for God's goodness. People will conduct themselves in ways that reflect God's nature. Paul offered this reminder: "You have been raised to life with Christ. Now set your heart on what is in heaven, where Christ rules at God's right side. Think about what is up there, not about what is here on earth" (Colossians 3:1–2 CEV).

When perfection comes, the imperfect disappears.

1 Corinthians 13:10 NIV

Let patience have its perfect work, that you may be perfect and complete, lacking nothing.

James 1:4 NKJV

This does not mean that people will act like robots in heaven or that they will not be able to fully express themselves. In heaven, people will be completely free to behave in the fullness of God's original intention. Their conduct will no longer be impaired by rebellion against God, and their attitudes will no longer be crippled by selfish considerations.

The Bible speaks of heaven as a place where humans will eternally learn and grow in their understanding. People in heaven are not omniscient, even though they will understand more than they ever did on earth, and they will continue learning and growing in heaven. People in heaven will know God fully for the first time, and it is this new, faith-fulfilling understanding that will free people to live without impairment or insecurity.

Points to Remember

- Heaven's citizens will be perfect human creations who are no longer saddled by disobedience and rebellion against God.

- People will know God personally in heaven. This firsthand relationship is possible because of God's completed work that allows people to be in heaven with him.

Check Your Understanding

- **What does it mean that humans will be perfect in heaven?**

Human perfection is not the same thing as God's perfection, but it is perfection nonetheless. It means that people will experience eternity exactly as God intended, with no impairment from disobedience or rebellion.

- **Why is it important to understand that people will still learn and grow in understanding in heaven?**

These concepts demonstrate that human perfection does not equal godly perfection. Instead, human perfection shows that people will forever enjoy and be stimulated by the experiences of eternity in heaven.

FAQ—Will the Physical Effects of This Life Be Evident in Eternity?

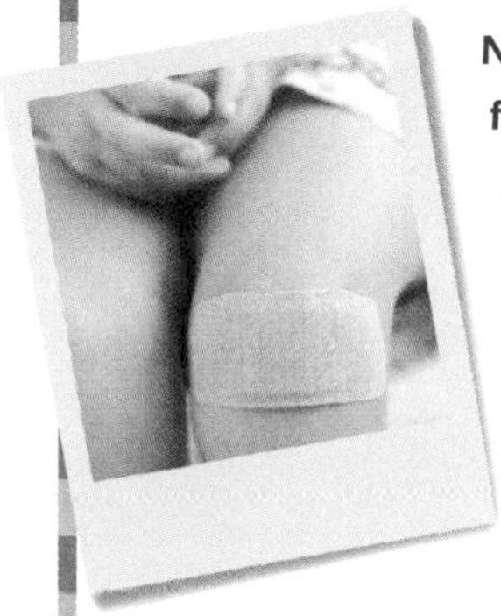

Nobody gets through life unscarred. Maybe it is a bonked forehead on a driveway as a toddler, a split chin at the swimming pool as a child, or an important surgery to remove a dangerous malignancy as an adult. Many people bear scars from dangers or elective procedures, while others are born with deformities or imperfections. The new, everlasting bodies in heaven promise to correct all these eventualities from the physical life, and they offer each person a peak physical form.

One of the unfortunate consequences of the broken relationship between God and humans is that people are sometimes marked by imperfections. Some people are born with chromosomal abnormalities that result in birth defects or cognitive impairments. Others may go through life with physical disabilities resulting from fetal malformation. It is reasonable to wonder whether these circumstances will be corrected in heaven.

> You are merely a clay pot shaped by a potter. The clay doesn't ask, "Why did you make me this way? Where are the handles?"
>
> Isaiah 45:9 CEV
>
> He personally carried our sins in his body on the cross. . . . By his wounds you are healed.
>
> 1 Peter 2:24 NLT

Life also offers many perils that don't result in death. People become disfigured or dismembered from wars, accidents, diseases, and foolish decisions. Many people who have endured these difficult challenges wonder if their scars will cross over with them into eternity.

The Bible declares that the physical body is corruptible, meaning that once a person dies, the body begins to decompose. The human body is entirely composed of natural elements (apart from surgical repairs or enhancements), and in time it will entirely decompose into natural elements.

When a person receives a new eternal body, it will be an entirely new creation, free from deformity or deficiency. In heaven, the blind will see, the deaf will hear, the paralyzed will run, and the infirm will be totally healthy. Scars, wounds, and other consequences from the effects of living the physical life will be left behind as each person fully enjoys the heavenly experience of their eternal, perfect, resurrected body. Every person will be forever satisfied with the body he or she receives in heaven.

Points to Remember

- Problems or shortcomings experienced with the physical body during earthly life are short-lived and temporary in the perspective of eternity.

- The physical features and characteristics that define a person in the physical life will likely be insignificant and not found in heaven.

Check Your Understanding

- **What happens to the distinguishing marks, scars, or physical characteristics of a person at death?**

A person's marks, scars, or physical characteristics will not follow through with a person to eternity. Those features were aspects of the temporary physical life that is known for its weaknesses and liabilities. Eternal bodies will be new creations.

- **How will humans be the same people in heaven if the bodies they have are different from the ones they used in the physical life?**

The physical body is not the essence of a person's identity. This essence is found in the spirit and soul of a person. A person's spirit is preserved and made holy, fit to occupy an immortal body in heaven that is free from imperfections.

FAQ—Will I Mourn Loved Ones Not in Heaven?

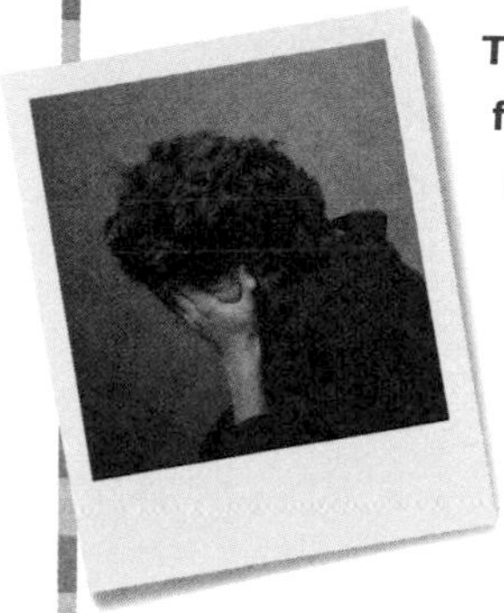

The prospect of heaven is indeed glorious—a place where friends and family reunite in the presence of God. The only stipulation is that everyone needs to trust God through faith in Jesus Christ. Yet the practical reality is that not all people reach the point where they have this faith. Not all people go to heaven. Inevitably, different decisions mean that families will be split and friends separated. The Bible speaks words of truth and perspective to this challenging premise.

It is a sad reality that not every person believes in God when his physical life ends. The Bible warns that many people choose the path that ends in eternal separation from God. Even though Jesus came to give all people eternal life in heaven, he does not force any person to accept the love he freely offers. This means that family relationships, friendships, and other close ties are destined to end when physical life ends.

> Anyone who neglects to care for family members in need repudiates the faith. That's worse than refusing to believe in the first place.
>
> 1 Timothy 5:8 MSG
>
> The One who sanctifies and those who are sanctified all have one Father. That is why He is not ashamed to call them brothers.
>
> Hebrews 2:11 HCSB

Jesus said that this would be the case, and he warned that his message would divide friendships and families because some people would believe his message while others would not. Jesus redefined the concept of family to include everyone who regards his message as truth, but he excluded from his family everyone who rejected his message.

He consistently used belief in his message as the standard of inclusion, and he distinguished believers from nonbelievers as "wheat and weeds," "sheep and goats," and "good fish and bad fish." He promised that his angels would separate each group from the other at the end of history. The angels would do this impartially, their decisions based solely upon whether or not each person believed or disbelieved the message of Jesus.

The Bible is replete with examples that family bonds can't ensure that the faith of one person transfers to a sibling or a child:

- Adam and Eve had faithful sons in Abel and Seth, but Abel was a murderer.

- Abraham became a man of great faith in God, but his son Isaac had to make many of the same mistakes his father made before growing in faith himself.

- Generations later, Israel's king Saul had no faith in God, but his son Jonathan showed deep faith through his friendship with David, who would ultimately replace Saul as king.

Every person is required to believe in God on his own, because belief cannot be inherited or bequeathed. Because of this, some people choose 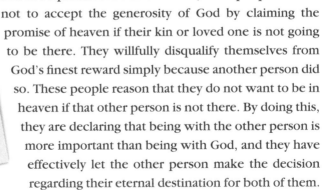 not to accept the generosity of God by claiming the promise of heaven if their kin or loved one is not going to be there. They willfully disqualify themselves from God's finest reward simply because another person did so. These people reason that they do not want to be in heaven if that other person is not there. By doing this, they are declaring that being with the other person is more important than being with God, and they have effectively let the other person make the decision regarding their eternal destination for both of them. The result is that these people will be eternally together, but apart from God and consumed by sorrow.

The promise that heaven will be joyful and complete even if it excludes nonbelieving loved ones is difficult to understand. People want to see their earthly relationships continue into eternity. God's plan is for Christians to use the opportunities they are given on earth to tell their family members about God's love and to pray for their families and friends. This is the Bible's promise: God "will wipe every tear from their eyes. There will be no more death or mourning or crying or pain, for the old order of things has passed away" (Revelation 21:4 NIV).

> He replied, "My mother and brothers are those who hear God's word and put it into practice."
>
> Luke 8:21 NIV

Heaven will likely include many surprises about who is included as well as who will be excluded. Heaven is a place of complete joy because everyone there will have made the necessary decision to trust God while living. It is heartbreaking to think that beloved friends and family may never experience the love of God in heaven. At the same time, it is reassuring that God's judgment is trustworthy, reliable, unchanging, impartial, and holy.

Myth Buster

While Jesus regularly emphasized that belief in his message was the criteria he used to determine who was included in his family, his earthly family was still incredibly important to him. Mary, his mother, was close to him his entire life. In fact, from the cross, as he was on the verge of death, Jesus commanded his apostle John to watch over the physical needs of his mother. James and 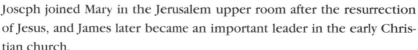 Joseph joined Mary in the Jerusalem upper room after the resurrection of Jesus, and James later became an important leader in the early Christian church.

Points to Remember

- The gospel of Jesus is as divisive as it is inclusive. Some families are split by it as members disagree over its truth while other families are united by it as they agree on its veracity.

- A person who opts to refuse the gift of heaven because a friend or family member disbelieves in God's offer effectively allows the other person to make the decision about eternal life for both of them.

- Heaven will be a joyful place because everyone who is there belongs there, and nobody will be excluded who should be there. Likewise, heaven will rejoice that God's judgment is fair and appropriate.

Check Your Understanding

- **How will heaven redefine the concept of family, and why will this be significant?**

Family in heaven includes every person who believed in God's promises during the physical life. This is significant because every person's understanding of family will expand to include many more people than what was understood to be family during the physical life.

- **Why won't there be mourning in heaven over family not allowed to enter heaven?**

The citizens of heaven will not mourn because heaven is defined by God's holiness, which is joyous.

- **Why is it important for people to share their faith if it cannot be inherited?**

Because faith is not something that is passed along by genes or legacy, it must be shared from person to person. Each person in a family individually determines whether to accept God's gift of heaven.

FAQ—Will I Recognize Friends and Family in Heaven?

Nobody appears the same at the age of forty as at fourteen. Likewise, every person experiences physical changes between forty and eighty. Differences in appearance can be affected by weight fluctuations, stress, work and family conditions, and numerous other variables. With people entering eternity at every possible stage in life, it seems unimaginable to be able to recognize one another in heaven. However, the hope of heaven is that the new body each person will have will somehow capture the essence of the individual and, accordingly, be easily recognizable by others upon reunion.

A great mystery surrounds the new, eternal physical bodies that people will receive in heaven. Many wonder if they will be able to recognize ancient relatives or old kin now wearing new eternal bodies. While the Bible does not answer these questions exhaustively, it does say that the eternal bodies given to humans will be incorruptible and in optimal form for God's eternal purposes. Moreover, it appears that regardless of how bodies appear in heaven, people will be able to recognize one another.

The Bible tells of a time when Jesus took some of his disciples up on a mountain, and his appearance was changed to how it will appear forevermore in eternity. He radiated God's glory. The long-dead Elijah and Moses suddenly appeared in the

We will all be changed, in a moment, in the twinkling of an eye . . . the dead will be raised imperishable, and we will be changed.

1 Corinthians 15:51–52 NASB

He was transfigured before them. His face shone like the sun. . . . And behold, Moses and Elijah appeared to them, talking with Him.

Matthew 17:2–3 NKJV

243

presence of Jesus. The apostles never had met these men, for they were separated by several generations. They had not seen pictures of them, for such technology did not exist. However, they recognized these men and knew their significance.

This foreshadows the likely possibility that there will be instant recognition of long-dead relatives and even an awareness of the identities of many people never met in the physical life. The essential being of the person as embodied in the soul and spirit will exude through the physical appearance in heaven far more transparently and recognizably than is possible in this current life.

Points to Remember

- Biblical precedent demonstrates that people will be able to recognize others in their resurrected form, even people they had never met in the physical life.

- The body a person receives in heaven will be optimal for its eternal purpose. It will represent the recognizable, essential personality of the individual forever.

Check Your Understanding

- **What happens to the distinguishing marks, scars, or physical characteristics of a person at death?**

A person's marks, scars, or physical characteristics will not follow a person to eternity. Those features were aspects of the temporary physical life known by its weaknesses and liabilities. Eternal bodies will be new immortal creations.

- **Why does it matter if a person's disabilities or impairments carry over to heaven?**

Most disabilities or impairments reflect the flaws of humans that are the consequence of the broken relationship between God and man. The reinstated wholeness of humanity in heaven is one of God's promises for eternity.

FAQ—Will My Marriage and Family Relationships Continue in Heaven?

When God created Eve, he did so with the purpose of uniting her with Adam as the parents of the first of countless families. Since then, the idea that an entire family will be in heaven together is an important concern for many people and cultures. The Bible teaches what will happen in heaven to families of this age. If misunderstood, these teachings could be considered troubling. With a correct understanding of the Bible, however, these teachings exhort families to look forward to a day when the entire concept of family is redefined.

✳

For many spouses, it is unimaginable that heaven offers a relationship that surpasses the marital relationship on earth. But that is exactly what Jesus promises. The Bible teaches that there will be only one marriage relationship in heaven, between Jesus and the citizens of heaven who make up "the church."

The biblical picture of marriage is that the bride and the groom become "one flesh." This means that two unique individuals share a spiritual intimacy unlike any casual relationship they have experienced. This experience is fully realized in heaven, when every Christian will have a genuine, intimate relationship with God. Every Christian will immediately understand God's sacrificial and provisional devotion, which will be deeper, broader, and more satisfying than any human relationship, even that of marriage.

We are all in a common relationship with Jesus Christ. Also, since you are Christ's family, then you are Abraham's famous "descendant."

Galatians 3:28–29 MSG

We know that we love the children of God, when we love God and observe His commandments.

1 John 5:2 NASB

Because of this, humans will relate more closely and happily in heaven than in the physical life. People will likely understand how they related to one another while living, and close relationships will still be appreciated appropriately. People who were respected in the physical life will still be respected in heaven. Parents' fondness for their children will continue in heaven, only more perfectly because the parents will appreciate their children with the eternal understanding of their relationships with God. All human relationships will be enhanced and made perfect because of the divine marriage that a person will experience with God.

Points to Remember

• Marriages between humans are not emphasized and do not exist in heaven. Instead, the better, perfect union between Christ and every citizen of heaven is celebrated.

• Human relationships will not only continue in heaven, but they will also be improved by understanding how everyone relates to God in a perfect union of love.

Check Your Understanding

▪ **What does it mean that people will not marry in heaven?**

Men and women will not be married in heaven because their deepest, most meaningful relationship will be with Jesus. People who were married in the physical life will rejoice in heaven that each is primarily united with God.

▪ **How will the marriage relationship with Jesus surpass the experience of human marriage?**

The marriage relationship with Jesus will allow all people in heaven to have perfect relationships with one another, whether they were kin or strangers in the physical life.

FAQ—Will I Be Able to Ask God Questions?

Human knowledge is limited, while God's knowledge is comprehensive and exhaustive. Many people have speculated that heaven will be an opportunity to sit down with God and ask questions about all the unknowns that were never fully addressed in life. The Bible teaches that human understanding will drastically increase in eternity, but people won't be omniscient like God. While questions to and about God are indeed interesting and curious, the promise of unsurpassed comprehension is a mystery that will be fully realized only in heaven.

The Bible describes the current physical life in terms of incomplete understanding and mysteries that are shrouded by faith. The promise of heaven, however, is that the shroud will be lifted and incomplete understanding will be made complete. Things that are unknown will be known, and things that are unclear will be clear and certain. The Bible describes the experience in heaven as "complete."

Humans in heaven will neither immediately nor eventually become omniscient. Humans will never become as all-knowing as God. Humans never have been, nor will they ever be, know-it-alls. With senses heightened, understanding expanded, rebellion and selfishness eliminated, and time forever extended, people will have a never-ending opportunity to learn and grow in knowledge and wisdom, however. These opportunities will likely extend back through human history. Even more so, though, these opportunities will extend forward into eternity as people explore and discover God's heaven.

Love is perfected with us, so that we may have confidence in the day of judgment.

1 John 4:17 NASB

Grow in the grace and knowledge of our Lord and Savior Jesus Christ. To Him be the glory both now and to the day of eternity.

2 Peter 3:18 HCSB

God created humans to have a personal relationship with them that spans eternity. A normal, reasonable expectation is that God will readily avail himself to answer the questions of his children in heaven. Whether clarifying historical facts, providing deeper understanding, or explaining meaning to those who seek it, God will gladly answer the questions of his dear people in heaven.

Points to Remember

• People will not be all-knowing in heaven. This is a characteristic of God alone.

• People will have all eternity to grow in their wisdom, knowledge, and understanding. People will have endless opportunities to learn from God and talk with God freely.

Check Your Understanding

▪ **Why is it important to understand that humans will not be all-knowing in heaven?**

It is important to understand that humans will not be all-knowing in heaven because omniscience is a quality of God alone. Humans do not become like God in heaven; humans will simply become perfect humans.

▪ **Why will people be able to freely ask God anything in heaven?**

In heaven, people will have a fully restored relationship with God. He will be continually in their presence, and they can speak with him the way a beloved child speaks with a parent.

FAQ—Will My Pets Be in Heaven?

One of the blessings enjoyed in this life is the faithful companionship of a beloved pet. Many people develop loving bonds of care and affection for their pets and experience deep sorrow when their pets die. People of all ages naturally wonder if they will experience a reunion in heaven with the family pet. While the Bible does not offer an explicit declaration on this subject, it does provide enough insight about the future of animals to give pet lovers and animal lovers an encouraging hope.

God clearly loves animals and holds them in high regard. When he created animals, he declared them to be "good," meaning they were perfectly suited for his eternal purposes. God established a special relationship between man and animals, having breathed "the breath of life" into both and created both humans and animals from the dust of the ground. Animals were created perfectly in Eden; when Adam and Eve "fell," animals experienced a consequence of that offense. God saw fit to protect animals through the flood by placing a multitude of the species on Noah's ark.

> Every created thing which is in heaven and on the earth and under the earth and on the sea, and all things in them, I heard saying, "To Him who sits on the throne, and to the Lamb, be blessing and honor and glory and dominion forever and ever."
>
> Revelation 5:13 NASB

The Bible teaches that there will be animals in heaven. The book of Isaiah speaks of wolves and lambs, leopards and goats, and calves and lions all living in unity. The book of Revelation speaks of horses. While there is no reason to think that this language is metaphorical, it is entirely reasonable to assess it as representative, revealing that heaven will include the entirety of God's menagerie.

The Bible does not reveal that the souls of animals are eternal; however, heaven will be the realm where all of what was corrupted on earth will be renewed and restored. While animals will not be resurrected the same way that humans will experience bodily resurrection, it is within God's capability to re-create animals or create new animals for heaven. Because heaven will be a place of perfect relationships, the bond between people and animals will be more profound than anything experienced in this life as all creatures worship God forever.

Points to Remember

- Animals were created for the use and enjoyment of people. That intent was not just for this life.

- Animal companionship should be appreciated as a gift from God. It is possible that your pet may one day be in heaven because it is a creature of God.

Check Your Understanding

- **How does the Bible's account of the creation of animals encourage animal lovers?**

God's design for animals from the beginning was for humans and animals to interact and to relate to one another. While that interaction was impaired because of the sin of Adam and Eve, God's original intent will be restored in the afterlife of heaven.

- **Why is it important to understand that animals will not be resurrected the same as humans?**

Jesus died for the sin of humans, not animals. Human bodies will be resurrected and made perfect in heaven. Animals do not need to be resurrected because of sin, but animals will be redeemed as a corrective blessing by the power of Jesus.

FAQ–Will Heaven Be Boring?

The common images are tranquil, serene, and quiet: heaven's citizens are all dressed in white robes, nestled in pillows of cumulus clouds. Every person in heaven has a halo, every person is winged, and every person is given a golden mini-harp with which to make music in everlasting songs of praise to God. For the person who isn't a musician, the image is anxiety-inducing. For anyone except the lazy, the entire scenario seems underwhelming and frighteningly boring. Thankfully, the promise of heaven is far more exciting than this bland, traditional premise. Eternity promises a full, never-ending experience for all its citizens.

The Bible promises that heaven will be a place where human senses are restored to their original creation specifications in order to fully appreciate all that eternity has to offer. Eyes will be able to see God, view the angels, and explore the heavenly creation. Ears will be able to hear the praise of angels and understand the voice of God that sounds with the power of a thousand waterfalls. Bodies will be perfect, never fatiguing or breaking or falling into disrepair. Joy will rise up from within a person and never ebb, diminish, or cease. People will have physical bodies that are perfectly suited to fully existing in a perfect environment.

Blessed are those who wash their robes, so that they may have the right to the tree of life and may enter the city by the gates.

Revelation 22:14 HCSB

When I saw him, I fell at his feet as if I were dead. But he laid his right hand on me and said, "Don't be afraid!"

Revelation 1:17 NLT

Beyond this, heaven, earth, and Jerusalem will all be new! An entire universe of heavenly creation awaits discovery, exploration, and development. Every person will be free and empowered to pursue the interests and intrigues of this everlasting environment. They will begin these opportunities with new friends, long-separated relatives, and never-before-known acquaintances. These opportunities will all be undertaken without any risk of danger or threat of evil, and all within the presence of God himself. Night will never fall upon this creation, meaning that the wonders will never cease. Glorious adventures that the mind cannot even perceive await those who are promised heaven because of the faith exercised in the physical life.

Points to Remember

• Heaven will not be boring. The idea that heaven will be mundane has been shaped from nonbiblical ideas of the afterlife.

• Heaven promises to be more amazing than anything experienced or available to be experienced on the current earth.

Check Your Understanding

■ **Why does it matter that your body will be different in heaven?**

It is important to understand that God gives each person a body that is perfectly made for heaven. Each person's body will be able to fully experience and maximally enjoy the heavenly creation.

■ **How will the heavenly realm be similar to and different from the current realm?**

Like the current realm, the heavenly realm will be created. Heaven will be eternally explored, discovered, and developed. Unlike the current realm, it will be completely void of evil or darkness. It will be a perfect environment for humans forever.

I have been established from everlasting, from the
beginning, before there was ever an earth.

Proverbs 8:23 NKJV

The Bible is called the Word of God because the
whole transcript is an inspired, faithful, and infallible
record of what God determined essential for us to know
about Himself, the cosmos in which we live, our spiritual
allies and adversaries, and our fellow man.

Walter Martin

Your kingdom is an everlasting kingdom.
You rule throughout all generations.
The Lord always keeps his promises;
he is gracious in all he does.

Psalm 145:13 NLT

The one who has spoken these things says,
"I am coming soon!" So, Lord Jesus, please
come soon! I pray that the Lord Jesus
will be kind to all of you.

Revelation 22:20–21 CEV

Books in The Indispensable Guide
to Practically Everything series include:

The Indispensable Guide to Practically Everything:
The Bible

The Indispensable Guide to Practically Everything:
Bible Prophecy and the End Times

The Indispensable Guide to Practically Everything:
Life After Death & Heaven and Hell

The Indispensable Guide to Practically Everything:
World Religions and What People Believe